Literature
and the Web

Reading and Responding with New Technologies

Robert Rozema
and Allen Webb

Foreword by Sara B. Kajder

Heinemann
Portsmouth, NH

Heinemann
361 Hanover Street
Portsmouth, NH 03801–3912
www.heinemann.com

Offices and agents throughout the world

Library of Congress Cataloging-in-Publication Data
Rozema, Robert.
    Literature and the web : reading and responding with new technologies / Robert Rozema and Allen Webb ; foreword by Sara Kajder.
        p. cm.
    Includes bibliographical references and index.
    ISBN-13: 978-0-325-02147-8
    ISBN-10: 0-325-02147-3
    1. English literature—Computer network resources.   2. English literature—Study and teaching—Aids and devices.   3. Literature—Study and teaching—Aids and devices.   I. Webb, Allen.   II. Title.
    PR35.R69 2008
    820.78'54678—dc22   2008010179

Editor: James Strickland
Production editor: Sonja S. Chapman
Cover design: Jenny Jensen Greenleaf
Cover photo courtesy of NASA at http://visibleearth.nasa.gov
Compositor: Newgen–Austin/G&S
Manufacturing: Steve Bernier

Printed in the United States of America on acid-free paper
12   11   10   09   08   PAH   1   2   3   4   5

*To all teachers
who continue to
experiment*

Contents

Foreword

Teaching to the Classrooms We Want to Have

Sara Kajder

There are twenty-seven students in third period, tenth-grade English at Western High School, all working to attain a passing score on the state assessment and all reading at least two years behind what counts as "on-level." The majority-minority nature of the school is reflected in the faces present in the classroom, as is the fairly significant economic divide between the middle-class and working-class families in the community. The classroom walls are bright with posters detailing the rubrics used to score student writing on the state assessments, samples of student work, and pieces of art. The curriculum is steeped in world literature, challenging students to read canonical texts starting with Achebe's *Things Fall Apart* and building to Homer's the *Odyssey*. Desks are arranged in small clusters of four to six desks turned in to face each other. One computer sits on the teacher's desk, connected to an LCD projector for full-class viewing of shared content. The shelves lining the walls of the classroom are thick with books.

As a teacher-reader, I require that anything I read stands up to the challenge of leading me to *re*-see and move my class in meaningful ways. Using the lens of this book, and the models that Robert Rozema and Allen Webb espouse as literature teachers of real students, I look into third period and see literacy in new and important ways. Yes, I see the ways that curriculum values alphabetic, print-based literacy—but I also am led to see the ways that multiple literacies are at play, both in our work in the classroom and in students' lives as readers and writers outside of their English class. Yes, digital technologies play an important role in this book—but at the core is what we value as English teachers:

We begin with what we English teachers already do well: engage students in the imaginative worlds of literary texts; teach them the skills of careful reading; show them how texts are woven into rich tapestries of history, culture, and biography; and lastly, encourage them to respond to literature in ways that are personally meaningful. (xxi)

What it means to read and write has changed, making this an exhilarating and daunting time to be English teachers. Robert and Allen understand this and offer a vision of how to teach with emerging tools in ways that amplify student learning. Further, they encourage us to see students in ways that acknowledge and value the multiple literacies that each brings into our English classrooms. They don't come to us as multimodal blank-slates or, as Robert and Allen offer, "our students are digital natives" (xx).

I believe, as do the authors of this book, that amidst the change and the speed of the development of new tools and technologies (e.g., Web 2.0 and Web 3.0 tools), our role as English teachers has never been more important. Our work is in helping students to engage with rich texts, wrestle with meaning, articulate their understanding, and use that "new" knowing to communicate with invested audiences. We have to know the tools enough to help them navigate the new landscape of audience and "connectedness." It isn't enough to say that kids will learn the technologies somewhere else. If we are teaching students to use the most powerful tools available to communicate their ideas and understanding, then technology simply has to play into our work. After all, technology would just be a pile of new hardware or software if it weren't for the promise in leveraging specific tools in ways that allow us to do something that we couldn't otherwise accomplish.

None of this work puts the computer between the teacher and students. Instead, as Robert and Allen offer, it creates openings. Think less about the computer as a barrier—and think more about how Web 2.0 tools make possible new ways of gathering, building community, and making meaning. Working with Web 2.0 tools in the literature classroom facilitates learning together and engagement in communities of practice that takes student work into robust and compelling places. We start in Chapter 1 in familiar turf—using word processing to collectively "deform" "Ode on a Grecian Urn" before launching on an insightful comparative study of different translations of Homer's *Odyssey*. The authors are quick to emphasize the added value of each of the tasks, and the richness and rigor of the instruction makes this abundantly clear. Each chapter works almost as an instructional think-aloud, letting us listen in on the decisions the authors make in developing activities and implementing the instruction. We move from tasks that are close to the "known" in a smart, intentional way to tools that allow for publishing to a global (and genuinely listening) audience.

This book is situated in a place that values teacher knowledge of the technologies used in our classrooms. In other words, if I ask the students in third period to use a blog to capture their responses to class reading, my work is really centered in how to teach students to write in a multimodal, online space that often plays by different rules than we use when writing in our in-class paper notebooks. I need to understand how blogs work, and, in the best case, have my own (like Robert describes in Chapter 3). I need to understand what good, rich reading and writing look like and how to communicate within a critical, connected community. And, I need to lead students to contribute within and facilitate a community, building what Tom Austin (cited by Pattison 2008) thinks of as "teamagers." This is teaching that is intentional, reflective—and that looks different from what I see when I look across many English classrooms. As teacher-readers, we are immersed in classrooms and teacher thinking—and this book contributes to changing our schema for what it means to teach English.

The authors continue to nudge us along, taking on increasingly sophisticated tools (e.g., wikis or weblogs) and tasks (e.g., literary analysis or development of authentic interpretive communities). At the core is thinking about the unique capacities of the tools alongside instructional methods that map directly into instructional challenges that we face daily in our classrooms. Podcasting exercises in Chapter 3 challenge us to think about the audience for our students' work. Book blogs and wikis lead us to consider what our students' knowledge and meaning making as readers and writers can do.

Teaching with Web 2.0 tools and twenty-first-century literacies isn't the latest in the long succession of fads or pendulum swings that so often mark our profession. This is teaching that values our students and the literacies they need to engage with and be successful in communicating in an increasingly wired, connective world, and that values, at its core, what we believe as secondary English teachers. Robert and Allen's energy is contagious as this forward-looking book leads us to teach in the classrooms we hope to create. Bigger than that—these are the classes that our students are hungry for us all to create. The tools might continue to change, but Allen and Robert's book will stay on my teaching shelf, challenging how I think about teaching third period—and the many classes yet to come.

▧ References

PATTISON, G. 2008. "It's Not About the Technology." www.fastcompany.com/articles/2008/03/interview-austin.html (Retrieved March 27, 2008.)

Acknowledgments

We are grateful to everyone who made this book possible: to Sarah Kajder, for her generous foreword; to Jeff Wilhelm, for laying the groundwork and inspiring us; to Lois Tyson, for responding to multiple manuscripts with clarity and grace; to Bob Rozema, for reading early drafts; to Lisa Rozema and Anne LaGrand, for integrating new technologies into their English classrooms; to all of our students, for allowing us to treat them as guinea pigs and willingly contributing their work; to Aldon Hynes, Jahan Aghadi, Kevin Jepson, and Timothy Miley, for their technical assistance on many of the projects described in these pages; to members of the NCTE Assembly on Computers in English and the CEE Commission on Technology for nurturing us and supporting us; to Robert Leneway, for collaboration on Preparing Tomorrow's Teachers to Use Technology grant; to the team members on the WMU Teaching Literature in Virtual Worlds Presidential Innovation Grant; and lastly, to Jim Strickland and the editorial and publication staff of Heinemann Press for providing excellent support throughout the writing and publishing of this book.

Introduction

Why Literature *and* the Web?

Robert Rozema and Allen Webb

E
nglish teachers love literature and believe in teaching it. In secondary schools we spend up to three-quarters of our instructional time teaching the writers we are care about—Shakespeare, Twain, Angelou—hoping to impart some of our passion to our students (Applebee 1993). In university English departments, literature remains at the heart of the curriculum, even as the canon continues to expand. English teachers know that reading literature takes effort, but it is effort infused with pleasure, with stimulation for the intellect and the imagination. We also know that teaching literature takes real work, as we push our students to engage imaginatively with stories; read texts closely; understand the social, cultural, and historical contexts of literary texts; and respond to texts in personally meaningful ways. In the past, teaching these complex reading skills involved books, pens, and paper. Today, the Web has given us a new set of tools for teaching literature, including digital archives, electronic discussions, blogs, podcasts, virtual realities, and more.

We believe these new Web technologies—when used in imaginative ways that build on what English teachers already know—provide some of the most promising ways to engage our students in literature. But let's be honest from the start. This book explores Web technologies, *not* because they are the latest trend or because student experience with computers will magically improve their chances in the global economy. Nor are we drawn to Web technologies simply because we know that young people spend an enormous amount of time online—though their fascination is something we shamelessly capitalize on. Instead, we are interested in these technologies and their application to literature teaching precisely for the same reasons that most English teachers are drawn into teaching. We want to enhance our students' love of literature. We want to excite them about reading the classic, multicultural, and young adult canons. We want to improve their reading skills. We want to extend their cultural knowledge. We want to develop their critical and creative thinking about themselves and the world. As you will discover, it is our allegiance to these traditional goals that underwrites all of our ideas for integrating technology into English classrooms and curricula.

We know that the rhetoric surrounding the word *technology* is both exaggerated and pervasive, often without much intellectual or academic sense. It is true that popular culture, video games, and the Internet are taking a toll on traditional literary reading; a recent study conducted by the National Education Association indicates that the number of students who become lifelong readers of literature is in dramatic decline (Bradshaw 2004). Yet we have seen that it is possible to use these same technologies to excite students about literature and improve their reading skills. Our approach, then, is to describe Web technologies in the context of the real and meaningful approaches that English teachers have taken for years, long before the invention of word processors or the Web.

Each of the new technologies we discuss in this book—digital text archives, electronic discussions, blogs, podcasts, feed readers, and virtual realities—will be examined in the light of what we believe are four key goals of literature instruction: (1) entering the story world; (2) close reading; (3) understanding the text's broader social, cultural, and historical contexts; and (4) responding to the text. Before we discuss what is possible with new technologies, we want to describe these stages, drawing on both research and classroom examples. These approaches to literature teaching provide our philosophical foundation and inform our integration of new methods and technologies.

■ Entering the Story World

Reading literature draws on and enhances the power of the imagination. Engaged readers often describe their experience as an escape into a world removed from their own. They speak of being *lost in a story*, immersed in the reality of what J. R. R. Tolkien called a "secondary world which the mind can enter" (1966, 60). W. H. Auden later borrowed Tolkien's term to distinguish between history, which records events occurring in the world, and poetry, which creates secondary worlds from words and imagination (1968, 49). As English teachers, we know that entering into the story world is critical to enjoying and understanding literature and to forming lifelong reading habits.

In *You Gotta BE the Book* (1997), teacher and researcher Jeff Wilhelm describes how readers encounter the secondary world of literature. Proficient readers, Wilhelm argues, engage literary texts in three distinct but overlapping dimensions: the evocative, the connective, and the reflective. In the evocative dimension, readers enter the story world, show interest in the plot, relate to characters, and visualize the story world. Wilhelm believes that many students have trouble in the evocative dimension—as they read, they somehow fail to envision the story in their mind's eye. Consequently these readers never advance to more sophisticated literary moves in the connective and reflective dimensions, such as elaborating on the story world, connecting literature to life, recognizing genre conventions, or questioning authorial intent (1997, 88). Drawing on his experiences with remedial students, Wilhelm suggests that literature teachers can make the events of the story more tangible by introducing dramatic and visual activities before and during reading, thereby helping students to enter the imaginative world of the story.

Wilhelm's students drew illustrations, created tableaux, engaged in readers' theater, conducted character interviews, and acted out role-plays based on the text. Literature teachers use these and other methods to prepare students to enter and begin to understand story worlds. Before reading Jack London's story "To Build a Fire," for example, a ninth-grade teacher might use a guided imagery activity to spur her students to imagine the weather in the Yukon Territories—and to speculate on how a person caught in a blizzard might stay warm. While teaching Toni Cade Bambara's "The Lesson," an American literature teacher may ask students to role-play a visit to an expensive toy store, with each student taking the part of a child from a different economic background. In the same way, a British literature professor might present a slideshow about eleventh-century Scotland, King James' ancestry, and the Gunpowder Plot in order to prepare her students for *Macbeth*. Teaching the same play, a high school teacher may require students to write about a time when they were tempted to do something they knew was wrong, anticipating one central theme of the play. All of these recognizable and commonplace strategies are meant to engage students in the world of the story.

The more difficult the reading level of the text, the further removed the setting and characters are from the lives of students, the more important that students are assisted in their early engagement with the text. When Allen taught Chinua Achebe's *Things Fall Apart* to second- and third-year college students, for instance, the difficulty of pronouncing African names was a stumbling block that prevented his students from getting involved in the story. As his students began talking about the characters, Allen encouraged students to practice saying their names aloud (e.g., "Ikemefuna," "e-kay-may-FU-na") rather than referring to "the boy from the other tribe who is adopted." Allen believed that something as simple as helping students pronounce these names correctly allowed them to connect to the characters more personally, while drawing their attention to Achebe's invocation of Igbo language and culture.

In a similar way, when Rob taught *Of Mice and Men* he wanted students to experience a life far different from their own—in this case, the hardscrabble existence on a Great Depression–era ranch. Early on in their reading, Rob asked his ninth graders to write letters from the perspective of one of the main characters. Adopting the voices and personas of Lennie, George, Candy, Curly's wife, or Crooks allowed students to empathize with them, fill in extratextual details about their lives on the ranch, draw parallels to their own experiences, and even begin realizing the larger themes of the novella.

Helping students to enter the story world is particularly important when students possess diverse reading levels and learning styles. And as we will argue here, English teachers should use every tool at their disposal to help all students develop the imagination required to immerse themselves in rich secondary worlds. Today many of these tools are digital, readily accessible via the Web, and already familiar to the majority of our students.

▪ Close Reading

In a 1993 study examining literature instruction in high schools with reputations for excellence, Arthur Applebee found that New Criticism, the dominant form of literary criticism from the late 1940s to the late 1960s, has heavily influenced literature instruction in American high schools, particularly in upper grade levels (1993, 124). The primary methodology of New Criticism, close reading, is at the heart of what we do as English teachers, even if we are not conscious of our New Critical assumptions. Simply put, close reading calls for careful examination of all of the text's formal components: images, figures of speech, narrative progression, and other verbal elements should be inseparable from the overall meaning of the text. If a work is well written, form and meaning will work together to create what New Critics called *organic unity*. Consequently, meaning is found within the text itself, not in external factors such as the biographical or historical context or the personal response of the reader. New Critics favored linguistically and structurally complex works such as the poetry of John Donne—the seventeenth-century metaphysical poet whose poetry relies on paradoxes, puns, conceits, and complicated formal devices.

While New Critical close reading has encountered resistance from literary scholars and teachers who find its philosophy too narrow, it remains an integral and necessary part of literature instruction. As every English teacher can attest, literary works typically contain complex or initially obscure passages that demand close and careful reading. This is especially true of poetry but also of difficult prose. For Allen, teaching high school seniors to read the anthology excerpt of John Milton's *Paradise Lost* became a fascinating challenge of working through the language of the text, subject by predicate, sentence by sentence, until they understood the literal meaning of the poem. Once they determined meaning at this level, they could move on to appreciate the astonishing majesty of Milton's language, which "with mighty wings outspread / Dovelike sat'st brooding on the vast abyss . . ." (1971, 20).

Another difficult and commonly taught text is *Heart of Darkness* by Joseph Conrad. As Rob discovered in teaching the novel to high school seniors, the text can be tough to grasp for many reasons, not the least of which is Conrad's elusive style. A non-native English speaker, Conrad relies on abstract Latinate nouns such as *abomination, indignation,* and *resolution.* He also favors adjectives with negative prefixes, often using them to describe what things *are not* rather than what they are. Moreover, the tale is complexly framed and told by a narrator, Marlow, whose storytelling approach is oblique at best. Rob and his students focused intensely on the language of the text, often proceeding as slowly as Marlow's steamer, even "translating" Conrad sentence by sentence until his meaning became clear—or at least somewhat illuminated "as a glow brings out a haze" (1990, 3).

Milton and Conrad—not to mention Chaucer and Shakespeare, Donne and Herbert, Eliot and Swift, Woolf and Wollstonecraft as well as a dozen others from the British literature canon alone—all require careful attention very much in keeping with New Critical methodology: the reader must slow down, focus on words and their relationships, examine denotation and connation, and decode the use of figurative and poetic language. We believe close reading is important for the interpretation of contemporary and multicultural literatures as well. In fact, close reading is perhaps the most important skill the literature teacher imparts to his or her students. As this book will illustrate, a wide range of digital technologies can assist in teaching and learning close reading strategies.

▨ Understanding Social, Cultural, and Historical Contexts

The study of literature today is characterized by theoretical approaches that emphasize what the New Critics saw as extratextual material. Marxism, feminism, new historicism, postcolonialism, and cultural studies—to name some of the dominant theoretical positions staked out by contemporary literary scholars—all interpret literary texts as strands of larger economic, social, cultural, and national fabrics. These frameworks suggest that a text cannot be considered in isolation from its context—indeed, the text is both the product of these external conditions and a player in reinforcing, complicating, or undoing established viewpoints. Hence from a postcolonial perspective, the writing and publishing of novels in nineteenth-century England was influenced, even financially underwritten, by British colonial expansion, and these novels usually reproduced imperialist ideas in their language, perspectives, and representations of colonized peoples.

Of course, literature teachers have always understood the importance of contextual information, even without taking or teaching specific theoretical stances. It is interesting to note, though, that secondary teachers *are* beginning to use critical theory to help students comprehend literary works. Texts such as *Learning for a Diverse World* by Lois Tyson (2001), *Literature and Lives* by Allen Carey-Webb (2001), and *How Does It Mean? Engaging Reluctant Readers Through Literary Theory* by Lisa Schade Eckert (2006) all demonstrate that critical theory can provide middle and high school students with powerful perspectives and useful vocabularies for interpreting literature. But even without an explicit study of feminist or Marxist theory, English teachers find it important to discuss the Victorian ideal of marriage while teaching *The Importance of Being Earnest*, or to spend time exploring how the working class was displaced and disenfranchised by the Great Depression when teaching *The Grapes of Wrath*.

Contextual information also helps students make sense of contemporary and multicultural works. We both teach the poetry of Sherman Alexie in our English education courses. Alexie, a Spokane Indian, has written loosely autobiographical poetry, short stories, and novels about growing up on a reservation in Wellpinit, Washington. When Allen teaches the poem "The Farm," his students examine the way Alexie combines Native American song chants and English. Allen asks what this hybrid form might say about Native American revival in the aftermath of genocidal invasion, spiritual and linguistic assault, and contemporary crisis. These questions take students and teachers into the complex cultural, historical, and political contexts of a literary text.

Contextualizing literature well, however, means much more than lecturing on the text's cultural background or supplying politically correct interpretations of history. When literature teachers help their students understand the contexts of literary works, they put these works into relationship with one another and help students see the connections between history and the present day. Literature teachers may draw together high and popular genres; consider the portrayal of different cultural groups; or examine philosophical and theoretical frameworks, standards of judgment, and the inclusion and exclusion of the particular curriculum materials. We need to organize instruction so that students engage with questions of context openly, creatively, and in ways that are meaningful to them. Again, instruction in this wide-ranging and complex domain of literary studies can be greatly enhanced, as we will see, though the use of Web technologies.

▪ Responding to Text

Louise Rosenblatt long ago argued that the meaning of a literary work is not simply inherent in it, but arises in a transaction between the reader and the words on the page. In this sense, interpretation is a highly personal and inventive act. "In a molding of any specific literary experience," Rosenblatt writes in *Literature as Exploration*, "what the student brings to literature is as important as the literary text itself" (1995, 77–78). For Rosenblatt, "what the student brings to literature" includes both affective elements—such as personality traits, memories, and emotions—and more cognitive elements, such as past reading experiences and knowledge of literary conventions. At the same time, interpretation is inevitably social, emerging from the complex cultural identities of writers and readers, as contemporary theorists like Stanley Fish and David Bleich have emphasized.

Drawing on the reader response tradition, English teachers create opportunities for students to respond in personal ways to literary texts, moving away from the one "right" teacher interpretation and toward an interpretive method that employs a variety of critical and creative activities. One of the first and most important responses to reading literature is class discussion. In a response-based classroom, teachers and students listen to each other and work in groups to develop interpretations of what they are reading. In such discussions, students learn through active participation—gaining confidence when their personal responses are heard and valued, and gaining insight and understanding as they learn from the responses of others.

Writing offers our students another means of personal response. In *How Porcupines Make Love: Readers, Texts, Cultures in the Response-Based Literature Classroom* by Alan Purves, Theresa Rogers, and Anna Soter (1995), the authors recommend a range of creative written responses to literature that go well beyond the traditional critical essay, including oral interpretations, process dramas, tableaux, story maps, sociograms, and illustrations. We have used many of these methods in our high school and university literature courses. In a unit on mythology, for instance, Allen required his high school students to create fictive newspapers focused on Norse myth cycle events. Working in small groups, students developed elaborate newspapers complete with hard news, gossip columns, sports reports, and personal ads—all based upon characters and events in the myths they were reading. In the domain of reader response, the implications for the usefulness of Web technologies may be the most obvious, as they offer students an incredible range of outlets for creative and critical responses to literary texts.

▨ The Web and Teacher Expertise

So far, in this shorthand way, we have identified four essential processes for literature teaching—entering the story world; close reading; understanding social, cultural, and historical contexts; and responding to texts—that are vitally important in any English classroom. We shouldn't forget that enormously important technologies inform even the most traditional English classroom. Think of the revolutionary power of the new technologies, even when those technologies were pen and paper, the chalkboard, and (that old-fashioned means of asynchronous communication) the book itself. We believe that new technologies are bringing about significant changes—if not as sweeping a revolution as the invention of the printing press, than a step-by-step evolution where books and the very best practices of literature instruction are not discarded but built upon, elaborated, extended, and renewed. That is precisely the promise and the possibility we wish to explore in the following pages.

But *why* use new technologies at all? If we already succeed in teaching literature without technology, or perhaps with only the bare essentials, why spend time and effort learning new skills? What if the digital tools we describe in these pages are just educational snake oil, as Clifford Stoll and other skeptics have maintained? And won't we need to learn new technologies again in two or three years, when the tools of today have grown as obsolete as floppy disks?

The answer, in short, is that the Web has become a basic part of our schools and our lives. The late 1990s and early 2000s saw unprecedented technology spending from the federal, state, and corporate sectors, with billions spent putting Internet-connected computers in every classroom. As a result, desktop computers, portable laptop carts, and high-speed Internet connections have become a reality for the vast majority of American public schools, even in schools with low-income and minority populations (Parsad et al. 2005). Even more promising, low-income and minority families are more likely than ever before to have Internet access at home. In 2002, more than two-thirds of low-income homes had Internet access, compared to only 45 percent in 2000 (Grunwald Associates 2003). While significant concerns do remain—their gains aside, low-income and minority households still trail the computer ownership rates achieved by high-income homes—real progress has been made toward digital equity.

But digital equity requires more than access to hardware, software, and the Internet. The technology explosion has put a premium on teacher expertise, and we have been hard-pressed to keep pace. Only twenty-one states include a technology course or assessment in their initial teacher licensure requirements, and about 15 percent of all schools nationwide have a majority of teachers who identify themselves as technology beginners (Swanson 2006). The issue of teacher expertise is especially critical in underserved schools. Middle- and high-income students, for instance, are also more likely than low-income students to have access to the Internet in multiple classrooms, where expert teachers can link technology with content-area learning (Grunwald Associates 2003).

Lack of teacher expertise is increasingly apparent as students come to our classrooms with a host of technology-related skills—ranging from using a cell phone, to sending instant messages, to posting pictures and music on social networking sites like MySpace and Facebook. Our students are digital natives. And while we can and should let them teach us their language, we should begin that encounter with at least a basic vocabulary. Consider the following statistics, taken from a 2005 survey conducted by the Pew Internet and American Life Project: 87 percent of American teenagers ages twelve to seventeen use the Internet; 51 percent of these use it daily. What are they doing online? Sending instant messages (75 percent), playing online games (81 percent), reading the news (76 percent), and shopping (43 percent) (Lenhart, Madden, and Hitlin 2005). Indeed, a teenager today spends more time surfing the Web than watching television (Grunwald Associates 2003). As teachers of this digital generation, we have an opportunity to take advantage of these behaviors, many of which involve literacy skills.

So where do we begin? We begin with what we English teachers already do well: engage our students in the imaginative worlds of literary texts; teach them the skills of careful reading; show them how texts are woven into rich tapestries of history, culture, and biography; and lastly, encourage them to respond to literature in ways that are personally meaningful. In all of these aspirations, Web technology is our ally. As we will argue in these chapters, it is exquisitely suited to help us teach English.

This book begins by looking at the Web as a vast storehouse of textual information. In recent years, the Web has become home to a wealth of electronic text archives, journals, databases, scholarly sites, and educational tools. (To cite one example, Google is currently working to make the contents of major research libraries available online.) In Chapter 1, Allen discusses how English teachers can use these resources to supplement or even replace course materials, enriching the traditional secondary canon and teaching their students key reading skills such as comparative textual analysis.

In Chapter 2, Allen explains his use of electronic discussions, a popular feature of course management systems such as Blackboard. While use of these subscription-based systems is on the rise in universities and secondary schools, many teachers feel underprepared to integrate them effectively. This chapter demonstrates how to set up and manage electronic discussions and describes the benefits that result from their use, both in and out of class. Allen also alerts us to one free course management system, Nicenet, which is easy to use and offers many of the features of Blackboard. And as always, literature is the center of the conversation, as Allen describes literature courses enriched and expanded by his use of electronic discussions.

Our third chapter explores more recent developments on the Web—namely, the emergence of Web 2.0 and its accompanying applications. As Rob explains in this chapter, Web 2.0 is characterized by dynamic rather than static content, collaboratively constructed and shared information, and easy-to-use applications. This chapter focuses on three Web 2.0 applications—blogs, podcasts, and feed readers—that are accessible to novices and experts alike. As in previous chapters, these new applications are aligned with the goals and practices of literature instruction.

Rob examines a collection of virtual reality technologies in Chapter 4. To be sure, none of these technologies involve the goggles or cybernetic implants envisioned by William Gibson in *Neuromancer* or Neal Stephenson in *Snow*

Crash, but they do entail simulations and scenarios that attempt to represent story worlds in virtual settings. Specifically, this chapter focuses on one particular application—the enCore environment—which we both have used to help students visualize, participate in, and critique literary texts. Rob also speculates on the potential of other experiential and immersive online worlds, including the massively multiplayer virtual environment *Second Life*.

Chapter 5 integrates the technologies described in the preceding chapters by suggesting two ways of establishing an online teaching presence—the class website and the class blog. We end the chapter with predictions about English language arts instruction in upcoming years, predictions drawn from our experience teaching in a wireless laptop laboratory at Western Michigan University, a learning environment we believe to be prototypical of future classrooms.

To make this book as useful as possible, we cover a range of Web technologies. Some of these have an established presence in secondary and university literature classrooms, and some are just beginning to appear on the scene. We hope our inclusions of older and newer applications make our book applicable to multiple teaching contexts. You may find some resources and tools mentioned in multiple chapters, embedded into different approaches for different objectives. For easy reference, we have included lists of Web resources at the conclusion of each chapter. All of the sites and applications we discuss in each chapter are listed, complete with URLs and short descriptions. We also know that teachers in many schools still lack equipment and support, so each chapter provides strategies for using the discussed applications with scarce or nonexistent technology resources. Finally, our conclusion explains how teachers can become Web advocates by using strategies to overcome technology resistance from colleagues, administrators, and parents; by adopting a bill of digital rights and responsibilities; and by becoming technology mentors in their schools and beyond.

It is our hope that this book prepares English teachers to use technologies currently available to them and readies them for future tools and innovations that can help them teach students the skills we all hold dear—reading and responding to literature.

Digital Literature: Electronic Archives in the Classroom

1

Allen Webb

In his imaginative short story "The Library of Babel," the Argentinean writer Jorge Luis Borges describes an infinite library with hallway after hallway, spiral staircases, and interconnected hexagonal galleries filled with books. The narrator has apparently lived all his life in the library "wandering in search of a book, perhaps the catalogue of catalogues" and, along with other "Men of the Library," he tries to understand the vastness and meaning of the collected volumes. At one point the men speculate that the library houses all the known works of the universe:

> When it was proclaimed that the Library contained all books, the first impression was one of extravagant happiness. All men felt themselves to be the masters of an intact and secret treasure. There was no personal or world problem whose eloquent solution did not exist in some hexagon. The universe was justified, the universe suddenly usurped the unlimited dimensions of hope. At that time a great deal was said about the Vindications: books of apology and prophecy which vindicated for all time the acts of every man in the universe and retained prodigious arcana for his future. Thousands of the greedy abandoned their sweet native hexagons and rushed up the stairways, urged on by the vain intention of finding their Vindication. These pilgrims disputed in the narrow corridors, proffered dark curses, strangled each other on the divine stairways, flung the deceptive books into the air shafts, met their death cast

down in a similar fashion by the inhabitants of remote regions. Others went mad . . . (1969, 79)

Borges' engaging and disturbing 1941 science fiction about life in an infinite library becomes a metaphor for the rapidly expanding and seemingly infinite library that now confronts us at our computer screens: the Internet. In at least one way, Borges was prophetic. Our civilization's libraries are being digitized with astonishing inclusiveness and speed. Jerome McGann, in his study *Radiant Textuality: Literature After the World Wide Web* (2004), argues that Western civilizations' entire cultural archive is moving onto the Web. For instance, the digital archive Early English Books Online purports to have digitized *every text* published in the English language before 1700—over 150,000 volumes. In the past, such resources were available only in specialized archives, often in remote locations and off-limits to the public. But what was accessible only to specialized scholars is now broadly available. Project Gutenberg currently offers over 17,000 free electronic books, with two million downloads every month. Relatively speaking, these are rather small archives and just the beginning. Google, in collaboration with the largest research libraries in the world (including Harvard, Princeton, Stanford, the Universities of California, Texas, Michigan, Virginia, and world libraries at Oxford, Madrid, and Germany) is well on the way to digitizing millions and millions of books. And there are hundreds more extensive online literary text archives where valuable and teachable works can be found. All of these texts are digitized; many include hyperlinked glossing and rich background information.

What does this sea change in the availability and delivery of literary texts offer to English teachers and students? Do we, like the men of the library in Borges' story, find ourselves the happy masters of all knowledge, or are we driven mad by an ever-increasing oversupply of information? Before you strangle someone on the divine stairways or throw your computer into an air-shaft, let us examine some possibilities for utilizing the virtual library of the Internet to extend and enhance the teaching of literature.

■ Teaching Poetry with Online Archives

Even before the Internet, textbooks for literature courses were simply getting bigger and bigger as they tried to include the expanding literary canon. One anthology I was looking at had 1,608 oversized pages and approached ten pounds. These anthologies are also expensive. A price tag of $80 is not at all uncommon—cheap, I suppose I *should* say, for so many great works of literature.

Last fall, a mix-up in editions suddenly meant that my introductory literature course would be without the monster anthology for at least a few weeks. Driven away from my textbook, I went online to look for reading material. What I found was an unbelievable depth and range of digitized literary texts. Most of the poems, plays, and short stories that were in the textbook were also available on the Web—along with much, much more. After a few hours of looking at the possibilities, I decided to teach the entire class using the amazing digital archives, literature sources, and texts found on the Web.

My course began with poetry. I was less concerned about specific authors, genres, or historical periods and more focused on helping students read carefully and closely while enjoying the works. I found extensive archives of classic and contemporary poetry—free, readily available, and at a wide range of reading levels. During our first class meeting, I showed students how to navigate sites and provided them with Web addresses of the Academy of American Poets, Poetry Archives, Bartleby, Project Gutenberg, American Verse Project, Library of Congress Poetry Resources, University of Toronto Poetry Online, British and Irish Poetry, *Poetry Magazine*, Poetry House, Poetry Archive, and the University of Virginia Modern English Text Archive. Our reading for the first three weeks of class entailed students surveying these archives, identifying poetry that appealed to them, and writing about those poems and how they use language and imagery. Many students sought out famous poets (including Robert Frost, Langston Hughes, and Emily Dickinson) and established classics (Shakespeare, Keats, and Wordsworth). Students also found, read, and enjoyed poetry by outstanding contemporary writers less familiar to me including Adrian Henri, Samuel Menashe, Polly Peters, Gillian Clark, Billy Collins, Alison Groggon, and many others. Many sites featured not only the poetic texts, but also recordings of poems read aloud (in the case of living poets, often by the poet). The Poetry Archive site, for example, describes itself as, "the world's premier online collection of recordings of poets reading their work."

Reading poetry from this diverse group of online archives meant that students were immersed in a world of poetry in a way that they simply could not be with a traditional textbook. So many of these sites are *alive*, connected to living poets and to poetry lovers. The Academy of American Poets (Figure 1–1), for instance, features a "National Poetry Calendar" where students can search for poetry events near them. This site also advertises poetry book clubs; accepts manuscripts from contemporary poets; gives poetry awards; produces a free podcast; offers a free newsletter; and provides reading recommendations, lesson plans, and resources for teachers. Other sites let students explore poetry in other ways, again far beyond what is possible in

FIGURE 1–1 *The Academy of American Poets*

Screenshot courtesy of The American Academy of Poets

printed text. The American Verse Project assembles volumes of American poetry published before 1920 and allows users to search for occurrences of words and phrases throughout the entire full-text archive—thousands of poems. The Poetry Foundation site includes searches by category, occasion, title, first line, and popularity. This site also features articles, audiovisual materials, links to poetry resources on the Web, subscriptions to poetry magazines, letters to the site, and more.

These poetry resources can be used by students and teachers at almost any level. They brought my introductory students into the world of professional poets, and lovers and scholars of poetry, so writing poetry or writing about poetry became a way to participate in an active community beyond the classroom. My students discovered that poetry need not be something frozen in a book. The freedom to move from site to site exploring the available resources was, in fact, empowering. Rather than simply taking the poems selected by the publisher of a textbook as my curriculum, my students were able to navigate the world of poetry, and the choices they made further developed their interest. As my students created links to their favorite poems and published these on their blogs (see Chapter 3 for more on blogs), they were in effect creating their own anthologies, inviting other students in the class to read their favorite poems and comment on them along the way.

My initial fear about reading poetry online, rather than from an anthology or textbook, was that students wouldn't give the language they viewed on a computer screen the same care they gave the printed word. I know that I prefer to have paper in front of me, and that I invariably write in my book—underlining and scribbling notes on words and lines. I suspect that people "read" the Internet in almost the same way they watch television commercials, letting many things go by without concentration. So I talked with my students about the kind of close reading I wanted them to engage in. In class, we used a data projector to display and magnify poetry so the whole class could read and discuss it. With a poem projected on the screen, I pointed at specific words, phrases, and even punctuation—modeling engaged, close reading. Of course, any of the poems found online could be printed out on paper, but somewhat to my surprise that neither happened nor seemed necessary. My impression was that students were able to read the digital texts with careful attention. That sense of reading with careful attention was magnified in the next assignment.

Digitized Texts and Textual Intervention

One of the remarkable things that can happen with online archives is that their digital texts can be copied and pasted into your word-processing program. This ability to take the words of a poem—or any work of literature—and put them into your word processor creates powerful close reading possibilities. The word processor lets us blend the actions of reading and writing together, and it makes rewriting and revision so much easier. When students have literary works in front of them in their own word processor instead of on paper or in an anthology, the potential possibilities for "scribbling" on the text are greatly amplified.

One day I projected an online version of Keats' "Ode on a Grecian Urn" onto the screen for class discussion. After reading the poem aloud, students identified interesting images, wrote about them, and then shared their thoughts. Each of the images we examined took us deeper into the poem's reflection on the message of the urn, the tension in the poem between organic life that changes, grows old, and dies, and the eternal beauty of art that the urn (and Keats too, we wondered) championed. We had an in-depth and engaging classroom conversation about this rich and wonderful work, though our text was only on the screen—a medium far more ephemeral than the urn itself.

Next I directed the students, who were stationed at computers, to copy and paste the poem into a Microsoft Word document. Looking for teaching ideas the night before, I had read the fascinating website of Keats scholar Jeffery C. Robinson, professor of English at the University of Colorado in Boulder. On a page hosted at the Romantic Circles website ("dedicated to the study of Romantic Period literature and culture"), Robinson describes his teaching experiments with "Ode on a Grecian Urn." He has the students do what he calls "deform" the poem, rewriting it into a new work. "When I deform a poem, I bring to it a highly selective consciousness and intervene materially in its existence, just as Keats does in encountering the Grecian Urn," Robinson states. His student Andrew describes the process:

> I slowly crushed the piece into different shapes. I broke it down and built it up again. I RETURN, RETURN, DELETE, DELETE, DELETE. Up and down the words skipped, lines jumping and leaping all over the computer screen trampoline.

When I tried Robinson's experiment in my own class, I was surprised by the ease with which my students took to the activity. For the first time this talkative class worked in silence. The only student comment came fifteen or twenty minutes into their busied activity when Anthony—a serious student— asked, "Can we add words?" Eventually I asked if anyone wanted to share the version they had created of the poem. One student read hers aloud. Meghan, a freshman, posted a version of the poem to her blog and shared it with the class. She told us that the poem that she was adapting from Keats's work was becoming a piece about spousal abuse, and she titled it, "Bound by Marriage, Embraced by Abuse."

> Bride of quietness,
> child of silence,
> Those unheard are sweeter,
> more endeared.
> Though canst not grieve,
> though thou hast not thy bliss.
> Play on, fair youth,
> thy song cannot fade.
> Forever wilt thou love.
> Never canst thou leave!
> More happy love!

(Forever breathing sorrow)
More happy, happy love!
(Forever panting, burning)
Sacrifice thy peace
Or silent be for evermore
And ne'er return.
Fair attitude trodden
By thy marble man
And by eternity.
In midst of silent woe
Truth doth tease you
But wasted beauty is all you know.

In his book *Textual Intervention*: *Critical and Creative Strategies for Literary Studies* (2006), Rob Pope talks about the way his students rewrite works of great literature in order to investigate not only language but also cultural and historical contexts. Meghan's version of Keats, for example, while playful and clearly a very different work than its source also raises questions about the gendered language of Keats' poem and the nature of his idyllic imagination of Greek romantic relationships. The ease and potential for textual intervention is greatly increased by the availability of digital texts. Students might cut and paste texts in such a way as to change genres, turning poetry into prose or vice versa. They could put a complicated nonlinear work into chronological order, or jumble the order to make its reading more interesting. The point is that the language of literature becomes something that students can get their hands and heads into, work with, manipulate for meaning, and thus come to see literature as actively created, interpreted, and reinterpreted.

Rewriting the Odyssey

I engaged in other experiments in close reading and creative writing in the next class assignment when my students read the *Odyssey*. One of the founding works of Western literature and a great read, the *Odyssey* is frequently taught at the ninth-grade level. Of course these students are not going to read the epic in ancient Greek. Since the Renaissance, the *Odyssey* has been translated into English over and over again by some of our language's most famous poets and scholars. Each translation is different, and reflects the literary and cultural sensibilities of the translator and their time. Some of these translations are justly celebrated. Perhaps most famous of those celebrations is the sonnet composed by Keats when he was twenty-one. John Chapman's translation of the

Odyssey—the first translation of the work into English—was put before Keats one evening by his friend C. C. Clarke, and they sat up together until daylight to read it, "Keats shouting with delight as some passage of especial energy struck his imagination. At ten o'clock the next morning, Mr. Clarke found the sonnet on his breakfast-table" (Seward 1909, 411).

> Much have I travell'd in the realms of gold,
> And many goodly states and kingdoms seen;
> Round many western islands have I been
> Which bards in fealty to Apollo hold.
> Oft of one wide expanse had I been told
> That deep-brow'd Homer ruled as his demesne;
> Yet did I never breathe its pure serene
> Till I heard Chapman speak out loud and bold:
> Then felt I like some watcher of the skies
> When a new planet swims into his ken;
> Or like stout Cortez when with eagle eyes
> He star'd at the Pacific—and all his men
> Look'd at each other with a wild surmise—
> Silent, upon a peak in Darien.

I can't promise that your students will respond with the same wonder— or poetic creativity—as Keats, yet studying different English translations of great world literature is certainly a rich and interesting way to engage with the text.

Looking online, I was able to find sixteen different English translations of the *Odyssey* available in digital archives, including Chapman's 1616 translation (at Bartleby.com—see Figure 1–2); Alexander Pope's in 1725 (Project Gutenberg, 17,000 free electronic texts); William Cowper's in 1791 (Bibliomania, 2,000 free online texts); Samuel Butcher and Andrew Lang's in 1879 (www .robotwisdom.com); Samuel Butler in 1900 (MIT Internet Classics Archive, 450 works); and a whole host of recent translations viewable at Amazon.com via the "search inside" feature. (Amazon itself is an interesting sort of archive, one where students can contribute their own comments and evaluations of texts.) I even came across an ancient Greek version with word-by-word trans-literation into English at the Perseus Digital Library. In finding some of these sites, I was helped by Jorn Barger's list of *Odyssey* translations at robotwisdom. com. I posted links to all these translations on my website, and in class we examined several translations of the first thirty lines of the poem. (For this assignment, see my site, www.allenwebb.net; the course is English 1100.)

FIGURE 1–2 *Bartleby.com*

Screenshot courtesy of Bartleby.com Inc.

My students were able to pick out substantial differences in the format and style of the translations, and when they looked closely at the word choice and phrasing they could also see how translations affected the reader's understanding of characters and events. At first students were drawn to the easier, more modern prose translations. But as we began to compare those translations with some of the older, denser, and poetic translations, I was astonished that the students kept saying that the older versions were "better" and that some of the newer translations seemed "lazy" (their word, not mine). Indeed, Alexander Pope's 1725 translation of the *Odyssey* emerged as the class favorite!

The students' first paper assignment on the *Odyssey* was to examine two or three of these translations from different digital archives in order to see how translation shaped the meaning of the work. I was delighted to see the careful readings that resulted from this activity. I quote from three student papers:

> Anyone trying to understand the poem [should] read more than one version to see the many layers in the original and expand the imagination to see what each line could have meant.
>
> —Rachel

> Subtle changes in word choice can produce different meanings, connotations, or a completely separate view of central characters . . . [Samuel] Butler's use of the word "ingenious" brings to mind thoughts of a quick-witted, even a cunning individual; one who never lacks a plan to get himself out of trouble. By describing Odysseus as being well known for "wisdom's various arts," [Alexander] Pope establishes a hero who is skilled and clever in multiple ways, rather than just quick on his feet.
>
> —Meghan

> Changes in the ideas and language of every society that has been exposed to the epic story have in turn altered the poem itself. These new versions may sound nothing like Homer's would have in the fields and villages of Ancient Greece, but the changes ensure that this work of art has lived on as long as it has and will undoubtedly live far into the future.
>
> —Andrew

Seeing many different versions of the same work also whetted student interest in the writing process. Students saw how translators had made subtle changes in words and phrases, and that even the *Odyssey* was open to revision and reinvention. Now I wanted them—even though they knew no ancient Greek—to do their own translation. (Before I had heard of "textual intervention" this idea was once suggested to me by Kim Bell, working with ninth graders at the Lake Forest Academy near Chicago.) I asked my students to choose a passage of the *Odyssey* that they found interesting for the images or events described, and then study several different English translations of those lines. (The original Greek text is available at the Perseus Archive.) Then by looking closely at different translations, they were to "interpolate" word-by-word meaning and create their own "translated" version of the lines. They could choose to make their version as contemporary as they liked and were free to write in either poetry or prose. Ashley wrote,

> Once you get going with this it isn't so difficult anymore. It's actually (dare I say it?) kind of, a little, teeny, tiny bit fun to do. Doing this definitely gives a significantly larger grasp of the literal story.

I certainly enjoyed reading their translations. Here is a sample of a very contemporary prose written by my student Alicia:

> When the beautiful red morning sun started to shine through the bedroom window, Telemachus woke up, showered and got dressed. He put his sandals on his feet, brushed his teeth, and put his sword over his shoulder before leaving the house looking handsome as ever. Then, he sent an announcement around to call everyone of the town together for a meeting. Telemachus does not travel alone, so he took his two cute little dogs with him to meet at the gathering place. As he walked by the people of the town to get to his seat, the most prestigious men even made space for him to pass through. Telemachus had a classy presence to him as he took over his father's chair.

Alicia clearly made the *Odyssey* her own. Having seen how translators modify the source text, she was comfortable making changes to convey the meaning as she understood it. I like the way her version sounds like contemporary speech, and I love the tooth-brushing! At the end of the semester, several students identified this creative translation writing as their favorite assignment.

Students can cut and paste from electronic texts and create their own commentary (or hypertext) with notes on specific words, characters, or ideas. They can make comments in different colors, perhaps using "track changes" to indicate thoughts of characters or to add to descriptions of settings. My students have tried many of these hypertextual interventions. One student worked with a collection of Garcia Lorca poems, hyperlinking them to each other around key images and metaphors and adding images that the poems referred to. Another student took Poe's short story, "The Tell Tale Heart," and, by linking from a number of words in the work, created a series of the inner thoughts of the narrator and provided a psychological justification for the murder. In a similar way, another student took Nathanial Hawthorne's short story, "The Minister's Black Veil," and, focusing on the character of Elizabeth,

FIGURE 1–3 *Literary Locales*

Literary Locales

More than 1,000 picture links to places that figure in the lives and writings of famous authors

Sponsored by the <u>English Department</u> at San Jose State University

Screenshot courtesy of Literary Locales

linked to a series of monologues she had written that retold the story from Elizabeth's point of view. A student created several different interventions into an Anton Chekhov short story, changing the social class of the characters in one, modernizing the tale in another, and altering the ending in a third. To each of these he added an explanation of the choices he made. Students can also insert pictures to create their own illustrated works—very effective with visually strong pieces such as the *Odyssey*. To find images for this exercise, visit the Literary Locales website (Figure 1–3), an archive of "picture links to places that figure in the lives and writing of famous authors."

These activities are not only possible with digitized texts, they are appropriate to the medium. Indeed, in *Radiant Textuality*, McGann argues that the digitizing of literary works is never just a recopying, but always a translation, creating new interpretations and additional layers of meaning.

■ Diversifying Cultural Perspectives

Lest you think that my students only work with traditional literary works, our next unit focused on reading digital texts from war, particularly the War in Iraq. We began by reading some classic war poetry and literature—all online—

including Mark Twain's "War Prayer," Winfred Owen's oft-anthologized "Dulce et Decorum Est," and Bertold Brecht's "War Has Been Given a Bad Name." But soon we examined the poetry of contemporary American soldiers and their families, published on sites such as the League of American Poets, Author's Den, Great War Literature, and Poets Against War. The fact that much of this poetry was contemporary, written in the last few weeks or months and detailing the real experiences of soldiers, gave this portion of the class relevance. It would simply not be possible to find this kind of material in even the most recent literature textbook or anthology.

From the poetry we turned to soldier's blogs. I directed students to Milblog ging.com, an index of blogs written by soldiers around the world, where students found detailed, provocative, and sometimes heartbreaking blogs about the soldiering life. The blogs represented a great variety of points of view on the war, but all were current—even up to the hours and minutes before class. Some included photographs and short video clips. During class discussion, I learned that my students had many connections to American troops stationed in Iraq. Two young women in my class had boyfriends there, one had a brother, and several more had friends.

Perhaps the most meaningful discussion took place when my student, Andrew, drew our attention to the Al-Jazeera news service site in English. Just as with the assignment to read different translations of the *Odyssey*, we began to compare different versions of the same news story, an exercise also possible with a feed reader (see Chapter 3). Treating the stories as digital texts, the students looked closely at the language of three different news stories. We were astounded by the dramatic differences in perspective and word choice.

As it so happened, the day we were comparing sites a lead news item was a horrific story reported by Al-Jazeera, BBC News, and CNN about the assault, rape, and murder of an Iraqi girl, her parents, and her five-year-old sister by a group of American soldiers. I asked the students what differences they could find. Looking at the details of the language, one student noticed "confusion about the girl's age" in the CNN article, which stated, "A Justice Department affidavit in the case against Green says investigators estimated her age at about 25, while the U.S. military said she was 20." However, the Al-Jazeera report provided a photograph of the girl's identity card showing her age as fourteen. "How does the different information about the girl's age affect our sense of the crime?" this student asked.

Another student noticed that information in the BBC News report provided an "explanation" for the soldiers' rape and murder and "blam[ed] it on the Iraqis" by mentioning that the soldiers were, according to the article, suffering "intense combat stress . . . left demoralized and emotionally drained by frequent insurgent attacks." The student noticed that even though eleven American soldiers took part or were present at the event, the CNN report seems to blame just one soldier with "an anti-social personality disorder." On the other hand, the Al-Jazeera site quotes the Association of Muslim Scholars, "an influential Sunni organization in Iraq," as issuing "a strong condemnation over the rape of the Iraqi girl and the brutal killing of her family by U.S. troops," referring to the Americans as "invaders," and claiming that the rape and killing, "show the truth of the ugly American face and shows that their claims of supporting humanity and liberation are false."

The close reading of detail, word choice, and nuance of meaning we learned in our comparative study of poetry and translations of the *Odyssey* were readily applied to a new kind of text—the online news report. Looking at the Internet for source reading makes possible the inclusion of texts, information, and news sources not usually available to students in the classroom. In this case, the class was able to study information from an Arabic news source and point of view and, by comparing it to American and British sources, raise basic and important questions about the information they customarily receive through more traditional media. Of course, our class discussed potential bias on all sides—why Al-Jazeera might want to quote the Association of Muslim Scholars and why CNN and BBC News reports would never describe Americans as "invaders" were among the questions we asked. But it was the inclusion of the Al-Jazeera reporting, made possible by the Web, that most prodded students to think critically about the language and detail of media coverage of the war and how U.S. actions might look different to other people around the world.

Teaching new literacies involves not only learning about and taking advantage of new materials (such as online poetry sites, digital archives, and scholarly electronic resources) but also helping students learn to think carefully and critically about what they read—mass media reports as well as literature. In this sense, teaching digital texts as part of new literacies offers us not so much a revolution as an evolution. We should be applying what we know about close reading and cultural studies to these new materials and, at the same time, expand our methods and approaches.

■ Digitized Mythology and Students Creating Textbooks

Another revealing experience I had using textual archives took place in a literature course I was teaching focused on literature from Africa—perhaps not the first place on earth you might think of as a source for electronic texts.

Indeed, the literature of Africa emerges from an enormous diversity of languages, cultures, and histories, and as we expand the canon of literature we teach, literature from Africa can be incorporated with students of any age. My class was going to read challenging contemporary African fiction, but I wanted the students to start by focusing on the oral traditions and storytelling that provide a foundation for later works, and that are relatively easy to read and culturally accessible. I knew that many of these students were planning to teach someday, and I hoped my class would give them texts they could use.

For these reasons, African myths, legends, and folklore provided a good starting point, but the paperback collections of African myths I looked at lacked enough variety or works that might appeal to students of all ages. On the Web, however, I discovered a rich source for African literature at the Internet Sacred Text Archive (Figure 1–4), "a quiet place in cyberspace devoted to religious tolerance and scholarship." This free site archives electronic texts about religion, mythology, legends and folklore, and occult and esoteric topics—including works from the ancient Near East to Zoroastrianism, from Buddhism to UFOs. Many of these texts are ideal for classroom use. The home

FIGURE 1–4 *Internet Sacred Text Archive*

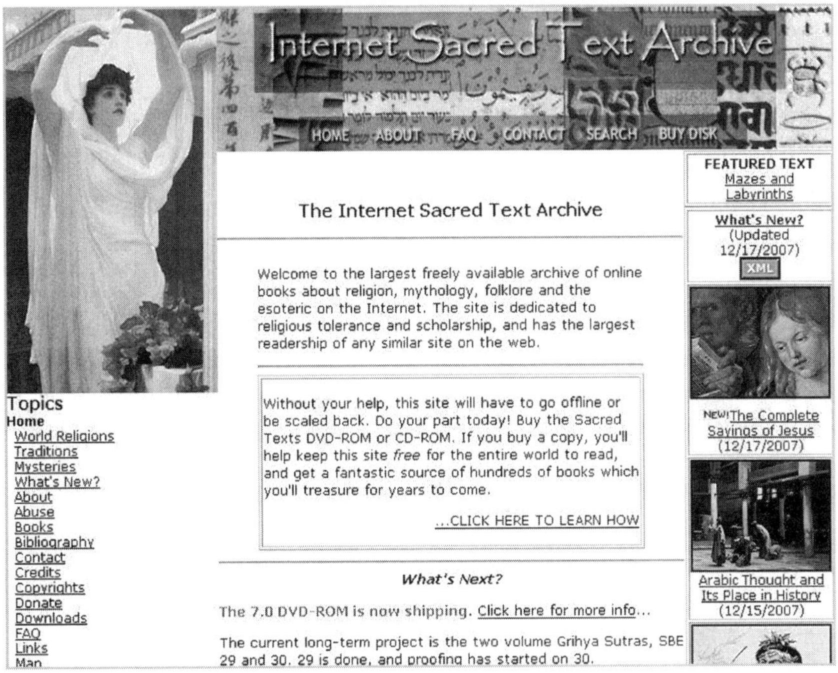

Screenshot courtesy of Internet Sacred Text Archive

page indicates that it gets a million hits *per day*. And it has a digitized, freely and openly accessible collection of major volumes of myths, legends, and folklore collected in Africa by European anthropologists from 1870 until 1940. Even the literature of Africa has a substantial presence on the Web.

I wanted my students to explore a diversity of African stories, find stories that they liked, and share those stories with the rest of the class. In this way, the digital archive they were studying would allow them to encounter a much greater variety of stories than they could from a large, dedicated anthology. I hoped that the students would find stories they enjoyed and take ownership of them, wanting to share them with their classmates and (some day in the future) with their own students. Thus I created the following assignment for my students:

1. Immerse yourself in African folklore from the Internet Sacred Text Archive. Read at least fifty pages from one or more volumes. Think about these questions: What are the characters like? What values do the stories express? What societies do you imagine that these stories come from? How were the stories collected?

2. Choose your favorite or most interesting stories, at least three or four, cut and paste them, print, and bring to class prepared to share with others.

3. Respond to our class' electronic discussion board conversation about African folklore.

On our class electronic discussion board (discussed in Chapter 2), I wanted students to develop enthusiasm for reading the folklore. I asked, "What are you learning about African folklore? Summarize a story that you find interesting and explain why." Although you likely won't recognize the stories the students discuss, let me share a few of their entries. These entries show how the works students found in this archive engaged their interest in African stories, started them wondering and speculating about the society from which the stories came, and led them to make comparisons between these stories and ones that they already knew from their own culture.

> Author: Katie
> 02-Sep 16:35
> The stories I enjoyed the most were ones that explained why certain things are the way they are today. A very simple one was "Why the Flies Bother the Cows," a Southern Nigerian folktale. It told of a feast to which all the domestic animals were invited. The cow was the largest so she sat at the head of the table and served everyone.

However, because the fly was so small she missed him. When the fly complained, the cow told him to look in his eye and he would get food later. The cow never fed the fly, so the queen said that, in return, the fly could always get his food from the cow's eye. The idea of flies bothering cows' eyes is so simple and something you normally wouldn't think about in such depth. It was interesting how much thought someone must have put into such a simple idea, but that also makes sense since the experience might be common in an agricultural community. A few other stories that explain why things are a certain way and are interesting to me are "The Story of the Leopard, the Tortoise, and the Bush Rat," and the Zulu stories "Why the Cheetah's Cheeks are Stained" and "Where Stories Came From."

Author: Amy
03-Sep 20:19
In the African stories I've read from the Internet Sacred Text Archive, I noticed a recurring theme similar to David and Goliath in the Bible, except with the use of animals. There are two sides to each story, one side is characterized by a lion, or some other "great beast," while the other side is characterized by a lesser creature who uses his wits to avoid being killed or maimed. I liked the story about the crocodile and his treason. This story is about a crocodile that lures all these animals to a place under the pretense of truce, which gets some of the animals killed. I also liked the story about the lion and the little jackal, in which the jackal gets out of being killed by using his wits and trickery. Both of these stories, incidentally, have a jackal in them. I'm getting the sense that some African cultures use the jackal as either a symbol of trickery or cleverness, depending on personal interpretation of the story presented.

Author: Jamie
04-Sep 15:50
When I think of folklore I think of a clear moral being involved and perhaps the reason I found "The Three Slaves" intriguing is the fact that the end of the story leaves me curious. It is about a polygamous marriage and which wife the husband will love the most. I finished the story wondering which wife will be after Dala's heart. (This curiosity is why, in my opinion, there should only be one wife! :). But this story also demonstrates such beautiful love, and the wives are willing to do so much for their husband. I liked this story mainly because it was different from the ordinary. I also like "Anansi and Turtle" because it was a story that depicted such

a clever mind. The spider thought he had so cleverly outwitted the turtle but instead the turtle outwitted the spider! I like it when the "little guy" wins! Overall, the stories are very enjoyable to read and are a good reminder of important lessons in our lives today. It's interesting to think that these stories have probably been handed down for generations and to see that the same underlying lessons are relevant today.

The comments here are typical—and there were many that were equally thoughtful and engaged with the reading. I believe that the interest the students show in this assignment comes partly from the independence and choice they experience. Students were able to browse through many, many stories and select those that attracted their interest. Although students tried to draw parallels with stories they knew or develop insights about Africa from the stories, the stories themselves were not difficult reading. This made it possible for students to read on their own in the archive without close support from the teacher.

Students can also create their own anthologies by cutting and pasting from digital archives (see the end of this chapter for ways of using text archives with limited or no technology resources). Assembled individually or by small groups, such anthologies can be annotated in many ways, linking to specific information about authors, movements, and traditions. This activity can also prompt students to reflect on how anthologies are created in the first place. Drawing on the Internet Sacred Text Archive, I assigned students to develop their own collection of African folklore and stories that they would use if and when they became teachers. Students were to choose an appropriate age range and develop a focused collection of stories, including information about what the stories are about and where they come from. They also developed study and essay questions for each story that went beyond recall to higher-level thinking. These assignments were posted on a website we created as a resource for students and teachers from kindergarten through college.

English teachers know that publishing is an important stage in the writing process, one that significantly increases student attention to their *own* work. My students turn in assignments that are almost always typed on a computer. Once their writing is in a word-processing document, it can be saved as HTML text, publishable on the Web. My work with archives has led me to involve my classes in the creation of websites of student work, and these sites in turn become resources—even archives, if you will—that are useful to a much larger audience. Publishing online involves students carefully considering a variety of dimensions of visual and textual expression, font size, background color, the inclusion of images, layout, and so on. Publishing on the Web also makes it possible to revise, update, and expand publications—over semesters and years—as groups of students contribute to the creation of valuable websites.

Students had a number of observations about the African folklore teaching units they had created.

> Author: Becky
> 19-Sep 15:49
> Having finished the teaching unit, I respect these stories so much more! At first glance they were amusing and appeared rather simple but I've learned a great deal! Having to come up with discussion questions and comprehension questions for all the stories really made me see how complex they are.

> Author: Emily
> 26-Sep 16:38
> I was very surprised by the folklore unit assignment because I actually enjoyed doing it! Although I have no intention of becoming a teacher, I was able to learn from my mother, who is a teacher in Mattawan [nearby school district]. I found it interesting to create a teaching unit that was pretty much aimed toward second graders. I spent a good amount of time creating activities and special pages for the students (and teachers) to use. Although it was a lot more work than was perhaps required, I really enjoyed creating the unit, and I know that I would not have been satisfied with my work, had I decided to omit the extra activities.

▪ Other Digitized Possibilities

Digital archives also lend themselves to other teaching and learning possibilities. Students can, of course, extend their reading in ways not possible with traditional textbooks. After reading a Greek or Shakespearean play, a Wordsworth or Dickenson poem, or a Twain novel as a class, students can find another play, poem, or novel by the same author. Students can search e-texts for specific characters, terms, or keywords to write analysis papers. They might want to find every occurrence of the word *sin* in Hawthorne's *Scarlet Letter*, or *devil* in Dante's *Divine Comedy*. There are many digital archives that provide online glossaries and extensive notations.

Many literary works were originally illustrated, and students can study these original illustrations and consider the relationship of illustrations and text. Examples include the Gabriel Rossetti Archive or original illustrations of *Huck Finn* found at the University of Virginia Electronic Text Center. In the

FIGURE 1–5 *Using text archives in the literature classroom*

Entering	Close Reading	Contextualizing	Responding
Explore texts independently	Study and create glossing for texts	Examine original illustrations, manuscripts, and variorum editions	Rewrite and intervene in the text
Choose texts of interest to read	Compare translations		Create hypertext commentaries
Examine illustrations and images related to texts	Search literary works for specific words and images	Study historical documents related to the text	Link images and text
		Explore additional texts by the same author or from the same time period	Create personal anthologies, class websites, and new online archives

William Blake Archive, students can examine all of his illustrated variorum manuscripts. Blake was both a poet and an artist (an engraver) and in this free, online archive, Blake's poetry and art are displayed together in ways that would simply not be possible in print. Scholars and students can examine the original engraved versions and examine how Blake's images enhance the text—a very interesting classroom project. They can look at side-by-side versions of the text published by Blake at different times and with different colors and effects. In online archives, students can examine large-scale images of original manuscripts, variorum editions, and facsimiles and compare these with modern or contemporary versions. This can take students into the fascinating history of the book and into the writer's process. This integration of the study of images with text is appealing to students at all levels.

In the introduction, Rob and I identified four key goals of literature instruction—entering the story world, close reading, contextualizing the text, and responding to text. Digital archives offer meaningful ways to meet each of these goals (see Figure 1–5).

◾ Looking Ahead: Copyright and Digital Texts

Each chapter in this book will conclude with a "Looking Ahead" section—a quick glance at what the future might hold for the Web technology the chapter discusses. It is fitting to begin by referring back to a remarkable essay published in the *Atlantic Monthly* in July of 1945. Before the dawn of computers, the scientist Vannevar Bush imagined the future of scientific research, in particular a machine he called the "memex," "a sort of mechanized private file and library . . . in which an individual stores all his books, records, and communications, and which is mechanized so that it may be consulted with exceeding speed and flexibility. It is an enlarged intimate supplement to his memory." Drawing on the technologies of his day he imagined "a keyboard and sets of buttons and levers," and the use of microfilm and dry photography that would make accessible

> books of all sorts, pictures, current periodicals, newspapers. If the user wishes to consult a certain book, he taps its code on the keyboard, and the title page of the book promptly appears before him, projected onto one of his viewing positions . . . Moreover, he has supplemental levers. On deflecting one of these levers to the right he runs through the book before him, each page in turn being projected at a speed which just allows a recognizing glance at each . . . Any given book of his library can thus be called up and consulted with far greater facility than if it were taken from a shelf . . . Yet the speed of action, the intricacy of trails, the detail of mental pictures, is awe-inspiring beyond all else in nature . . . Wholly new forms of encyclopedias will appear, ready made with a mesh of associative trails running through them, ready to be dropped into the memex and there amplified. The lawyer has at his touch the associated opinions and decisions of his whole experience, and of the experience of friends and authorities. . . . Thus science may implement the ways in which man produces, stores, and consults the record of the race. (2006, 56)

What Bush called a "suggestion" of the future is, in fact, a prophecy; yet even in Vannevar Bush's inspired vision, the scientist still works merely with a personal library. Consider now the staggering scope of all the knowledge of research libraries becoming digitized, made available to anyone with an Internet connection. It is no wonder that publishers of textbooks and anthologies are running scared and creating their own websites, some of which allow teachers to create their own textbooks by selecting from an online index.

Some people point out that copyright law may have limiting effects on the distribution of texts. Copyright laws do attempt to limit access, though all books published before 1923 are free from any copyright restrictions. Technically books published after 1923 are under copyright until seventy years after the death of their author. This is a matter of special importance when it comes to including more recent multicultural literature in the curriculum, though poetry and other shorter texts by multicultural writers have already found their way onto the Web. Readers take note: teachers and professors do have additional freedom in the classroom under "fair use" laws, extended to distance learning by the 2002 TEACH Act. Google, in the effort to digitize library holdings described at the outset of this chapter, is finding ways around copyright rules—claiming that it is only creating a "card catalogue" and limiting, for the time being, access to books not in the public domain to snippets. Indeed we predict that copyright may not be able to maintain those limits for long. Copyright laws become ineffective when digitization makes unauthorized usage enormously easy. Moreover, reductions in the cost of producing and distributing information are likely to make copyright a less valuable source of income.

Writing about the Google book digitization program in the *New York Times* on August 31, 2006, James Harding predicts that "Google Does Book Reading a Huge Favor":

> Google may have just done for book-reading what email has done for letter-writing. Yesterday the Internet search engine started making classic, out-of-copyright books available to download and print free. The service makes available to everyone the dusty pages of old tomes that once were reserved only for those with privileged access to the likes of the Bodleian library in Oxford and Harvard University in Cambridge, Massachusetts. Google likes to boast that its mission is to organize the world's information, but it is doing something better than that: it is democratizing it . . . Google's service will be a boon to researchers and students. It will enable people to browse bits of books and, it must be hoped, cultivate more interest in reading. For the publishing industry, it will ultimately foster demand. And, in the process, it will reinforce one of the more extraordinary features of the "lean forward" technology that is the Internet, namely that it is generally not dumbing us down but lifting us up. (2006)

Inevitably, digitized books will increasingly become part of the core curriculum of English language arts and literary study. Our texts will also become more multimodal than ever before as websites, images, film, graphic novels, podcasts, and historical texts and materials are ever more easily incorporated into teaching and learning. We believe that these new materials, and the ease of access to traditional materials now available online, will not dilute the need for more careful reading skill. For years teachers have brought various complaints against textbooks and anthologies, not the least of which is expense. Yet literature no longer exists only in books. Learning to read, explore, analyze, work with, and contribute to free online texts will become a common feature of teaching and learning in our English classes. As this chapter shows, we are now able to extend the range and depth of available reading, facilitate close and creative engagement with literary language, and foster student choice and commitment. Bringing digitized texts into our courses opens up possibilities for deep and relevant historical and cultural studies. Helping students to find their way—and make meaning—in the infinite "library of Babel" is likely to be one of the hallmarks of English teaching in the twenty-first century.

Using Text Archives with Limited or No Technology Resources

In the past decade, we have seen hardware and software stream into schools and universities, sometimes outpacing support systems and the professional development that should accompany them. Now it is rare to find a public school that does not have a high-speed Internet connection, unusual to find a community college without at least one computer lab, uncommon to find a university without some wireless access, and atypical to find a student completely unfamiliar with sending email or surfing the Web. And yet we know that teachers across the country *are* still underequipped, and *are* teaching students who have never used a computer, much less explored a text archive. For teachers in these circumstances, we suggest the following ways of using text archives:

- Text archives can be accessed in the one-computer classroom and projected for reading and discussion. This is especially useful for rich archives with visual images or recorded readings of poetry.

- Specific works can also be printed and copied for students to read.

- The textual interventions I describe here can also work with a pencil and printed copies of a poem instead of a word processor. In this way, students could still compare different translations and study literary works beyond those included in their textbooks or library.

Web Resources Mentioned in Chapter 1

Academy of American Poets (www.poets.org) offers hundreds of essays and interviews about poetry, biographies of poets, almost 2,000 poems, and many audio clips.

Al-Jazeera Magazine Online Edition (www.aljazeera.com) is an independent news media organization established in London with a focus on the Middle East.

American Verse Project (http://quod.lib.umich.edu/a/amverse) is an electronic archive of volumes of American poetry prior to 1920.

Author's Den (www.authorsden.com) is an online community of authors and readers.

Bartleby (www.bartleby.com) is an Internet publisher providing free access to literature, reference, and verse.

Bibliomania (www.bibliomania.com) offers free literature with more than 2,000 classic texts.

British and Irish Poetry (www.thepoem.co.uk) features contemporary poetry from Britain and Ireland.

Gabriel Rossetti Archive (www.rossettiarchive.org) is a hypermedia archive of the complete writings and pictures of Dante Gabriel Rossetti, one of the leading writers and painters of late nineteenth-century England.

Google Book Search (www.books.google.com) allows searching text in books from libraries and publishers—sometimes full text is available, in other cases snippets.

Great War Literature (www.greatwarliterature.co.uk) is a comprehensive collection of printed and electronic study guides on World War I literature.

Internet Sacred Text Archive (www.sacred-texts.com) is the largest freely available archive of electronic texts about religion, mythology, and folklore.

The League of American Poets (www.poetryamerica.com) publishes poetry online and in anthologies.

Library of Congress Poetry Resources (www.loc.gov/rr/program/bib/lcpoetry) is a comprehensive guide to locating poetry resources available on the Library of Congress' website.

Literary Locales (www.literarylocales.com) provides more than 1,000 picture links to places that figure in the lives and writings of famous authors.

Milblogging (www.milblogging.com) provides a large index of military blogs in thirty countries.

MIT Internet Classics Archive (http://classics.mit.edu) features full texts of over 400 works from ancient Greece and Rome.

Perseus Digital Library (www.perseus.tufts.edu) is a source material digital library in the humanities supported by the Classics department at Tufts University.

Poetry Archive (www.poetryarchive.org) describes itself as the "world's premier online collection of recordings of poets reading their work."

Poetry Archives (www.emule.com/poetry) offers over 5,000 searchable classical poems, includes a discussion board.

Poetry House (www.thepoetryhouse.org) is a gateway site to international poetry.

Poetry Magazine (www. poetrymagazine.org) is a journal dedicated to a "desire to print the best English verse which is being written today."

Poets Against War (www.poetsagainstwar.net) "continues the tradition of socially engaged poetry by creating venues for poetry as a voice against war, tyranny and oppression." Site includes poetry archives, newsletter, and information about poetry readings.

Project Gutenberg (www.gutenberg.org) provides over 20,000 downloadable books in its free catalog.

Romantic Circles (www.rc.umd.edu) is a refereed scholarly website devoted to the study of Romantic-period literature and culture supported by the University of Maryland.

University of Toronto Poetry Online (http://rpo.library.utoronto.ca/display/index.cfm) includes over 3,000 English poems by 500 poets from the Old English period to the work of living poets today.

University of Virginia Electronic Text Center (http://lib.virginia .edu/digital/collections/ finding_digital.html) is an online archive of humanities materials that includes more than 70,000 texts and 350,000 images and collections in modern English (from 1500 to the present), early American, American poetry, African American, and many more.

William Blake Archive (www.blakearchive.org) is a hypermedia archive of the writing and printing of William Blake, sponsored by the Library of Congress and supported by the University of North Carolina.

Reading and Responding Online: Electronic Discussions

2

Allen Webb

And George raised the gun and steadied it, and he brought the muzzle of it close to the back of Lennie's head. The hand shook violently, but his face set and his hand steadied. He pulled the trigger. The crash of the shot rolled up the hills and rolled down again. Lennie jarred, and then settled slowly forward to the sand, and he lay without quivering. George shivered and looked at the gun, and then he threw it from him, back up on the bank, near the pile of old ashes. (106)

And, yet, out of it all, over and above all that had happened, impalpable but real, there remained to him a queer sense of power. He had done this. He had brought all this about. In all of his life these two murders were the most meaningful things that had ever happened to him. He was living, truly and deeply, no matter what others might think, looking at him with their blind eyes. Never had he had the chance to live out the consequences of his own actions; never had his will been so free as in this night and day of fear and murder and flight. (239)

Two quite different literary depictions of murder from frequently taught texts—depictions that students react strongly to and want to discuss and debate. If you haven't already recognized it, the first is from the violent ending of John Steinbeck's *Of Mice and Men*. In an online threaded discussion, ninth graders in Lisa Rozema's English class discuss George's decision to shoot Lennie, debating and learning from one another:

Marie: I think George is one of those guys who would try and do anything to save a friend. I think he shot Lennie out of love and while he was doing it, he believed it was the best thing for his friend.

Sam: Part of me realizes that Lennie probably would have just caused trouble in the next place they went. Nonetheless, if I were George I would never be able to live with the fact that I killed my best friend, and I'd probably feel lonely the rest of my life.

Kristy: I think that George was taking the easy way out. He has the possibility right away when he sees Lennie to tell him to get up and run, but, instead, he gets him on his knees like a public execution. It was just cruel, painless, but cruel.

Justin: In the Ten Commandments, God doesn't say, "Do not murder unless it's for a friend and you do it painlessly." No. God said do not murder, period! Don't you think that God might be a little wiser than we are?

Tim: Regardless of the Ten Commandments, I totally think that George made the right decision when he shot Lennie. It was not an act of cruelty. I can't even imagine how much love it took to pull the trigger and end his life like that. He was trying to protect Lennie from what was going to happen to him.

Jordan: I really, really don't know what to say about this topic. The issue is so multifaceted that we can bring up all the opinions we want but we'll never find a definite right or a definite wrong. One, rather fatalistic side of me says, "It was fine to kill Lennie. He most likely would have been cruelly and painfully murdered by Curley." The optimistic side of me cries, "They had a chance to escape to freedom and perhaps make their dream a reality." You could only want the best for Lennie and George.

As they debate the moral complications of the end of the novel, these fourteen-year-old students simultaneously explore their thoughts about friendship, personal choices, religious belief, and the power of love. Writing in this electronic forum is a collaborative inquiry into the meaningful connections the students have made with literary characters.

The second quote is from Richard Wright's 1939 novel *Native Son*, a story of racism and violence in America's inner cities. Whereas George and Lennie were homeless migrant workers in California, Bigger Thomas is a teenager in Chicago's ghetto, employed as a chauffeur by the wealthy white man who owns the apartment building in which he lives. One evening, Bigger unintentionally kills the man's daughter, Mary Dalton, when—trying to help her—he is frightened by the possibility of being caught alone with her in her bedroom. Bigger attempts to frame Mary's communist friends for the murder, and he goes on to commit robbery and another killing. Living in a deeply racist world, Bigger has all along felt confined, tense, and angry. George throws the murder weapon away, but breaking the law leads Bigger to feel free and powerful for the first time in his life. In another electronic conference, my students wrestle with the difficult question of how to judge Bigger's actions, and talk to each other with a frankness they might not have risked face-to-face:

Charles: I believe that the central question of *Native Son* is: How much of what happens is Bigger's responsibility and how much is society's? When does it cease to be the criminal's fault for taking the actions and start to be society's for creating the environment that produced the criminal?

Scott: I have to agree that it was Bigger's environment that caused him to do the things he did. Not only was society as a whole condemning him, but his own family and culture were doing the same. Monique made a good point in class by noting the importance of support from one's home environment. Yes, it's true that Bigger made his own decisions; however, those decisions, violent as they were, became Bigger's only sense of control. During those times and those times only, was Bigger truly in control of his life.

Sarah: I'd like to respond to what Monique and Scott said about needing support from home. I personally think Bigger got a lot of support from home. His mother was behind him completely when he finally got a job. The only reason she criticized him was because she knew what he needed to do, and that was to stop robbing people and doing something good. She was doing the best she could.

Ecaroh: I have lived as an observer of the system every day in my neighborhood. It seems to me once you got in, there was no way out. All the friends I have who were in the system are either still in, back to old crimes hoping not to get caught, or a few even dead. As a young black male, I feel the system is just another way of contributing to making the black male extinct. I have yet to see the system rehabilitate anyone I know.

Ondraya: I think for Bigger to rob Blum, a white man, was the ultimate sin yet the ultimate high at the same time. To go through with the plan would show that Bigger wasn't letting the white man control him totally, which, in essence, would be Bigger's only way of showing his hatred of the white man.

Meredith: I don't understand that kind of oppression he [Bigger Thomas] experienced and the intensity of it, to actually make a person feel that level of hate. Bigger hopes for a different world. He makes references to people being blind, and to a dream he has about the sun melting away everyone's color. I guess I am not in a position to judge what he feels as right or wrong.

Notice how both of these electronic discussions of literature are both similar to and distinct from in-class face-to-face discussion. As with class discussion, in the electronic forum students draw on class reading and conversation. The capacity to formulate thinking in writing; the added time to respond; rereading classmates' comments and reviewing the whole discussion before (and after) making their own contribution; the fact that none of the students are "called on" but all are responsible to contribute—these circumstance of electronic discussion add richness beyond what is possible in the classroom. In the conversation above about *Native Son*, we see the students (and they can see each other) move from assigning judgment, to understanding character, to reflecting on related life experiences, to recognizing limitations of their own understanding. Using the new tool of electronic discussion, the students explore fundamental questions of violence, judgment, racism, and social justice relevant to the novels and to their own lives.

■ My Beginning in Electronic Discussions

Before I started to use electronic discussions in my classes, I was skeptical of the hype about computers in the teaching of English. I had seen simplistic programs that provided students with scripted writing prompts or marched them through skill-and-drill grammar exercises or canned questions about reading. These software programs seemed, if anything, a step backward toward less thoughtful forms of teaching. Then I attended a Michigan Council of the Teachers of English state conference and heard Cynthia Selfe talk about using computer-aided electronic discussions programs with her English class. Selfe argued that students who were reluctant participants during in-class discussion often became active during online discussions. Selfe pointed out that women and minority students in particular often feel intimidated in white, male-dominated classes and were more likely to share ideas in a forum that gave them the time to formulate and express their ideas without being interrupted or stared at face-to-face.

It has always been important to me to create inclusive discussions—like those above addressing *Of Mice and Men* and *Native Son*—so Selfe's argument struck home. It wasn't computers I was excited about: it was the intense, meaningful, and sometimes wonderful discussions that we had in class about the literature we were reading.

The discussion of *Native Son* was from the first threaded discussion I set up after the conference. (Threaded discussions are ones in which students can respond not only to the initial question, but also to each another's comments and responses.) The class I was teaching included both white and African American students, and one challenge was getting them to talk to each other about the racially charged issues. The white students were often the first to speak, and at the outset I wondered if the African American students felt safe in the classroom. I believe that the excerpts from both discussions suggest that Selfe was right: even students who might be reluctant to share their thoughts face-to-face are more likely to contribute in an online forum. Participating at home or from computer labs outside of class, my students were willing to take on even difficult topics. As the class progressed, I saw that online discussions enhanced student confidence, which spilled over into class conversations, building a sense of trust and community. Thus my first experience with electronic discussion made it clear to me that it might have a great deal to offer English teaching.

My sense of the potential value of online conversation was also sparked by watching my daughter Jessica come home from middle school and go straight to the computer to spend hours and hours using Instant Messenger to write fast-paced, informal notes to her friends. This was certainly good for her typing skills, she learned the shorthand language of informal online conversation, and it may have been good for her social development as well. More importantly, I found myself wondering how to harness Jessica's energy for interactive writing and academic learning. Middle school students writing like crazy to each other after school, college students opening up to each other across racial divides as they talk about literature—these two experiences drew my attention to the possibilities for using electronic discussions in my teaching. This chapter will share some of what I have learned as I have experimented with electronic discussion in the teaching of literature.

▦ Selecting Online Discussion Tools

I use the expression *electronic discussion* to refer to a variety of online conferencing and course management tools that are both available commercially and free online. These forums can be synchronous, in which participants log on and communicate with one another in real time (as in the instant messaging my daughter used, chat rooms, or multi-user environments such as *Second Life*). Or they can be asynchronous, where participants post messages over an extended period of time and others respond (as in the threaded discussions I used with *Native Son* or *Of Mice and Men*, message boards, or bulletin boards). In general I have found that asynchronous forums are more likely to develop in-depth thinking and complex student interaction than chat, though a chat function can be useful for holding smaller student group meetings and one-on-one conferences (and, as Rob will discuss in Chapter 4, they open interesting possibilities in virtual world activities now emerging).

An electronic discussion resource that I have used extensively with my students is Nicenet, a 501(c)(3) nonprofit educational organization (see Figure 2–1). Nicenet is a free educational site accessed by more than one mil-

FIGURE 2–1 *Nicenet.org*

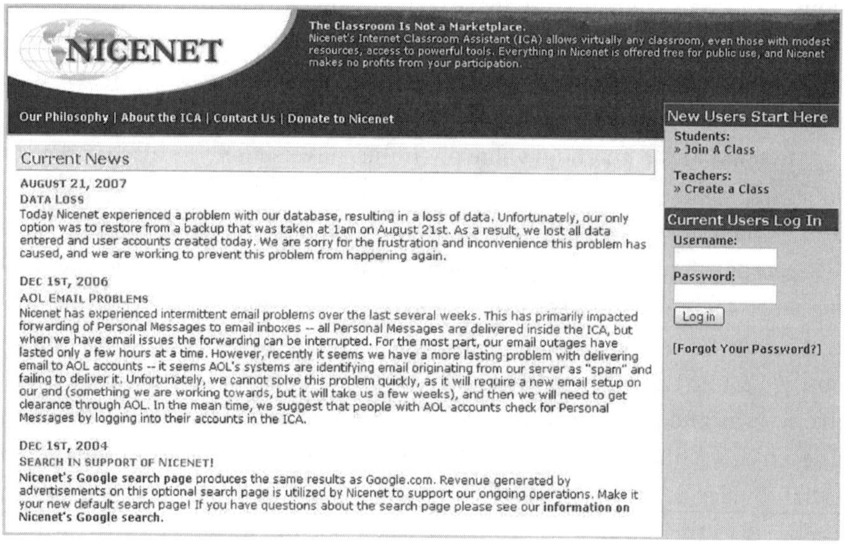

Screenshot courtesy of Nicenet

lion people since it began in 1998. Setting up a class on Nicenet takes about two minutes. You provide a user name, password, name for the class, and contact information—and that's it. Nicenet then gives you a unique password, or *key*, that you in turn give to your students so they can create user accounts and access your course. You could set up a class right now by following the *Create a Class* link from the Nicenet site. Because the class key is required to enter the conversation, Nicenet is completely private—the only people who access it are the people you give the password to: your students, other classes, or specific visitors you invite. Better still, Nicenet is entirely Web-based; neither you nor your technology administrator needs to install or manage any software. Nicenet offers a number of features, including tools that allow teachers to upload documents, provide links to Web resources, and facilitate email between teachers and students.

Other programs offer more complete classroom management options. Blackboard is a popular commercial product that charges a fee and is in use at many universities and, increasingly, in public schools. Blackboard and WebCT (which merged in February of 2005, and have partnered with Google scholar since October 2006) include both chat and bulletin boards, as well as threaded discussion tools. They also allow students to turn in work, take online tests or quizzes, and check their grades. Desire2Learn is a similar commercial product. Moodle, rapidly emerging as an open-source alternative to Blackboard, is free and can be downloaded onto almost any server. Moodle has also been adopted by many schools and universities. Collaborative writing spaces called wikis often include discussion tools. The wiki I have used, Wikispaces, lets users create webpages and participate in threaded discussions.

No matter which of these options you choose, an electronic discussion allows you to create lead items—sometimes a question, sometimes a response to the text—that your students can respond to over the next few days or even weeks. The student comments about *Native Son* occurred in a discussion item I created that was part of a much larger discussion with multiple items that we used throughout the course. As the students become familiar with the technology, I encourage them to create new items as well. While I may demonstrate how to use the electronic discussion during an in-class lesson, my students are usually assigned the discussion as homework, so the time they spend posting comments and responding to others typically takes place outside of regular class time. Of course, electronic discussions can also be used as an in-class activity. Students will engage intensely in these discussions—perhaps in ways that are more focused than in a regular face-to-face conversation.

▪ Integrating Electronic Discussions into Class Activities

Since I typically have students write responses to questions in our threaded discussion after they have done the assigned reading but prior to talking about it, their writing helps to clarify and develop their thinking and prepare them for our regular in-class discussion. The electronic conference has many advantages over simply asking for this writing as a homework assignment. The writing is shared with all class members and is interactive, so students can agree or disagree with, expand or elaborate on points made by their classmates. Since the date and time of all entries is posted, the teacher knows exactly when entries were made and the assignment completed (see Figure 2–2). As I read the electronic conference before our class discussion, I keep a piece of paper in front of me and jot notes on comments made by specific students. I take note of what students are interested in, and what they see and respond to in the text. I assess what the students know and what they are having difficulty understanding. Since all students contribute to the forum, my sense of how well they have understood the reading is based on much more knowledge than would arise from simply accepting volunteers or calling on students during class. By using the electronic discussion in this way, I am able to begin in-class discussion by drawing on the wealth of student thinking before class has even met.

FIGURE 2–2 *A threaded discussion in Nicenet*

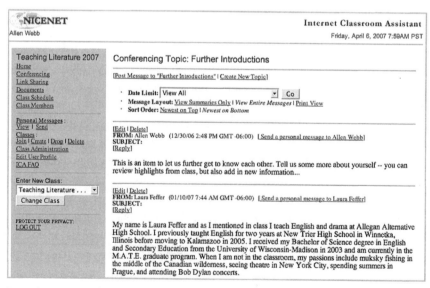

Screenshot courtesy of Nicenet

One of the most important aspects of an electronic discussion is the way that topics can continue to be developed—perhaps weeks, months, or the entire semester. In addition to having discussion topics related to specific assignments, it is possible to post items that raise questions that will have continuing relevance, and it is fascinating for teachers and students alike to see these conversations grow over time. If the conversation remains lively, students will return again and again to the topic. Every time students enter the electronic forum, they can tell where there are new comments that they have not read. I may have some discussion items that are supposed to be responded to *before* class on a particular day. At the same time, these items may be returned to by students *after* class as well. Now these online written commentaries become a place where students can see their own and their classmates' ideas evolve. The conversation often moves easily from the electronic to the face-to-face.

Just as in the classroom, a teacher using an electronic discussion needs to establish a sense of community, set clear guidelines and expectations for student participation, set a high intellectual level for the conversation, and participate in and mediate the conversation effectively. Researchers on electronic communication refer to an online disinhibition effect, where many people find it easier to share thoughts online than face-to-face. Participants in an electronic discussion may feel safe since they are typically alone when writing, are not physically visible to other members of the conversation, and there is a lag between writing and receiving a response. Teachers can thoughtfully use this disinhibition to help students develop confidence in their ideas and participation.

While I make careful efforts to call on and involve *all* students during in-class discussion, inevitably some students are more active participators than others. Supplementing class with an online discussion shifts the balance of participation. Students who are fairly quiet in class may emerge as major players in online discussion. An interesting example was JoAnne—a shy young woman active on the volleyball team, but so quiet in class that I had begun to wonder if she had special needs. As our electronic conference progressed, JoAnne emerged as one of the most frequent, and sharpest, contributors. During in-class discussion, other students frequently referred to JoAnne's ideas—ideas they had come to know only from her participation in the electronic discussion. Even though JoAnne uttered hardly a word in class, she emerged as a major discussion participant—even a class leader!

Every teacher has had the experience of leading a discussion and finding that interesting side topics are raised. As discussion leader, you often have to make quick decisions about whether or not to follow any number of potentially interesting and important conversational paths. With an electronic conversation as a supplement to class discussion, I frequently find myself commenting in class, "You are raising an important and interesting issue. I don't want us to follow that issue right now, but I think we should follow it up in the electronic discussion." Then I create a new item in the electronic conference that builds on that topic. This conversation may then continue outside of the classroom, but still very much inside our class at the same time. In this sense the electronic conversation lets me honor student ideas, concerns, and contributions in a way that I wasn't able to in the past.

As students become more familiar with electronic discussions, they become better able to make decisions about creating their own items—something I usually allow a few weeks into the class. Often their items are every bit as pertinent to the class as any item I could come up with. I remember a student once creating "An item to discuss the articles that our teacher assigns us to read but that we don't seem to have time to talk about in class." (In addition to being a good conference item, it was also a clue for me to alter my teaching practices!) In my methods class preparing future English teachers, students have repeatedly created items about their experiences substitute teaching. While substitute teaching is not a topic I address in my class, it is a topic of interest and importance to my students and thus, I believe, a good addition to the electronic discussion. Granting students the freedom to introduce discussion items often helps me better understand my students' responses and interests; listening in can help me refocus and improve my teaching.

I assign a lot of group work in my classes—and one of the greatest challenges for students is finding times that they can meet outside of class to engage in conversation and carry out required group work. An electronic conversation can provide an important vehicle to facilitate small-group conversations. If the tool is asynchronous, then students don't even need to meet at the same time—they can enter into the electronic discussion at a time that works best for them, read the postings of other group members, and respond. Since it is easy to cut and paste from a Word document into an electronic forum, students can share their papers or writing with their group and get feedback. An online electronic discussion creates an ideal format for group response and editing activities.

Setting Boundaries

Given their social interest and energy, electronic discussions are ideal for middle school and high school students. I have learned that I need to have specific guidelines as to how, and how often, students are expected to participate in

FIGURE 2–3 *Strategies for leading electronic discussions*

- Because body language and voice tone cues are not present in an electronic discussion, it is especially important to remind students to be respectful and appropriate in their comments.

- Emoticons (colon followed by right parenthesis for a smiley face, etc.) can be used, but students will learn that these emoticons are superficial, lacking the subtlety or impact of voice or facial expression.

- I tell students that before they *flame*—react angrily or personally—it is a good idea to reread the entire discussion item to be certain that they really understand the context of other students' remarks.

- Sometimes a student may write something that you as a teacher consider inappropriate, either in terms of content or tone. Nicenet, Moodle, Blackboard, and most other discussion forum programs make it possible for the teacher to remove student comments, and I have done so—though surprisingly rarely. When I have done this I have written an email to the student concerned and explained my actions.

the electronic forums (see Figure 2–3). Of course these expectations need to be modified depending on the level of students you work with. With my students I need to be clear about expectations and hold them accountable. I explain that certain questions that I post require responses by specific times and dates and will be checked off in my grade book—these are for conversations intended to take place before class discussions, for example. I typically expect students to visit the electronic forums twice a week for half an hour each visit. Of course they can do this on their own time. As the time and date stamp on their postings reveal, often they visit the conference late at night or, more rarely, early in the morning. I also tell my students that I expect a certain number of words overall entered into the conference per semester.

I developed my contribution expectations for the electronic discussion board after using the tool for a couple of semesters and getting an idea of what was possible and appropriate. Would you be surprised if I said that I have had students in college courses required to write over 7,000 words (about twenty-five typed pages) over the course of a semester in a typical electronic class discussion? Many students exceed the requirement; in a class I recently finished teaching I had only asked for 6,000 words (it was a shortened seven-week summer class) but the *average* student wrote over 8,000 words—and one student wrote over 11,000 words! This is pages and pages of focused and interactive writing directly related to the topics, themes, and reading of the course. While this writing may take the place of certain daily homework assignments, it is always over and above what they are assigned to write in their larger papers and projects.

In order to generate productive discussions, teachers need to be thoughtful about the kinds of questions they ask. An online conversation about the impact of rhyme scheme on poetic meaning is going to be harder for most students to sustain than, say, a discussion of the depiction of women in a literary work and how it compares to other works in the syllabus or contemporary life. I have found that an electronic discussion works best when the literary works are in a curriculum that puts them into dialogue with each other, and with historical, cultural, social, or political issues that relate the literature to its context and to students today. I have written elsewhere about developing cultural studies curriculums for secondary and college literature teaching (Carey-Webb 2001). A cultural studies approach provides issues tied to the literary work that students will want to sink their teeth into and grist for ongoing conversation and discussion.

An electronic format can be time demanding for the teacher. I remember one of my colleagues, Jil, getting started with electronic conferences in her class. She was so swept into the activity that she was checking the electronic discussion board several times a day just to see what new thoughts her students had posted. Two semesters later she had burned out with the activity. "Allen, it is just too time consuming," she told me.

As a teacher bringing an electronic discussion into my course, I am careful how much time I spend in the electronic discussion. While I do respond to student comments in an interactive way, trying to model the kind of comments and inputs that I want my students themselves to make, I have realized that students do not need me to participate with them in every conversation or to be an ever-present arbiter or commenter. It is more important for me to set the expectations and guidelines and then step back from some of the commentary, conserving my efforts and (in effect) turning the discussion over to the students.

■ Using Electronic Discussion to Teach Literature

Given the importance of class discussion in English courses, the medium of the electronic conference is especially pertinent to our subject area. Just as with in-class discussion, there are many ways that electronic discussion can facilitate the teaching of literature. Of course, I have used electronic discussions for the whole-class discussion of literature, where we scrutinize the meaning of a text, with the discussions of *Of Mice and Men* and *Native Son* that head this chapter. I have also pasted poetic texts in whole or in portion into our electronic forum to foster close literary readings, a method discussed in Chapter 1.

An electronic conference can also include links to texts and websites outside the conference where students can study related materials as they write their entries. Nicenet, for example, allows teachers to post links with the *Share Links* feature. I used this feature to allow students to jump from our electronic discussion to a scholarly Shakespeare site that featured annotated versions of his plays. This site allowed close analysis of the language of the play, which in turn informed our electronic discussion. Some teachers include links to information related to the literary text, including historical, cultural, and biographical information; even online critical or scholarly articles can be used. All of these resources help students contribute to the threaded discussion in more meaningful ways.

Electronic discussions are appropriate with all levels of literature students. In addition to working with younger students, I have used an electronic discussion with adults in a graduate seminar reading Charlotte Bronte's *Jane Eyre*—a novel I have taught many times to high school seniors. The electronic conversation began before our class meeting, with one student posting a short paper to which the other students responded. To give you a flavor of the kind of conversation that can take place with older and advanced students, I provide you a strand (much pared down), which I have selected from that discussion. As you read through these few comments, notice how the students develop ideas from one another, how their thinking can be as complex as in a formal literary analysis, yet as flexible and collaborative as an in-class discussion.

> Author: Kelly
> 05-Oct 15:14
> In the evolution of these binary oppositions, the gothic component—the mysterious and grotesque—insinuates itself throughout the novel: the ghosts, the white forms, the moon, the chestnut tree, the disembodied voices, and their settings. At Thornfield the gothic element culminates in the revelation of Bertha Mason in whom we see Jane's antithesis. Bertha is the binary opposite of womanhood in general, as viewed in the 19th century, with its dogma of division between home and the economic world, male/female spheres of responsibilities, woman's moral superiority, and the idealization of motherhood . . . Few gothic characters, including Mary Shelley's *Frankenstein*, have embodied bestiality as well as Bertha. Did Brontë require such a character device to rip asunder the spiritual union

between Rochester and Jane? Or was Brontë reaching deep inside herself, tearing away social constraints, to give us a portrait of a female's raw, animal desire unfettered by conscience or intellect?

Author: Heather
06-Oct 12:31
I would like to comment on the binary opposites of Jane and Bertha and the topic of Jane's struggle between self-determination and socialization. Jane tries outwardly to conform to what is expected of her. She attends school and upon leaving takes up the position of governess. She realizes that she has few options for her life. She can be seen as in the process of being "successfully socialized." Yet, underneath her outward exterior Jane seethes with emotions and feelings it would be unseemly for her to express. Hence, the character of Bertha who is beyond social norms because she is mad and therefore free to act out her aggressions through rage and destruction. We see a literal manifestation of Jane's repressed feelings through Bertha's actions.

Author: Nat
07-Oct 22:34
Kelly's and Heather's response highlight the fact that *Jane Eyre* is a complex novel . . . one could plausibly argue that *Jane Eyre* is a novel of repression. Jane is incredibly restricted by her status as an orphan, her position in relation to her Aunt and Cousins, her social position due to lack of money, her roles as student and governess, and her subscription to Christianity. It seems that Jane's actions and responses are constantly circumscribed, not just by outside forces, but also by her own beliefs (which are of course the product of her upbringing). Jane's early attempts to break with convention result in severe punishments and separation from society. She soon learns to toe the line, and as she matures she adopts an extremely conservative stance. Her refusal to become Rochester's common-law wife, based on her immutable religious beliefs, is a prime example of the repression of her deepest desires.

Author: Jason
08-Oct 15:33
I was enthralled with the character of Bertha and it seems from some of the responses that others were as well. I was thinking *Frankenstein, Dr. Jekyll and Mr. Hyde*, the id and ego, etc. So I decided to do a little research and I found out that there are three popular interpretations of Bertha's character. (1) Bertha is representative of

Victorian marriage where the woman is encaged. Bertha then, tearing the wedding veil of Jane, is portraying the harsh feelings that Jane possesses toward marriage internally—feelings of servitude, etc. The question also becomes, is Bertha mad and therefore needs to be imprisoned, or, does her imprisonment (i.e., marriage) make her mad? (2) Rochester's marriage to Bertha represents the British Empire's cultural and economic exploitation of its colonial subjects. We know that Bertha is "creole" which means she is of mixed descent (possible European born in the colonies). Locking Bertha in the attic could be seen as Britain trying to lock in the attic different cultures that it politically holds dominion over. (3) This is the one that most people talked of already, that of Bertha being Jane's alter-ego—Bertha as Jane's manifestation of frustration, fear and outrage that Victorian women are at a loss to express since there is no socially acceptable outlet for such expression.

As these graduate students explore the role of the character Bertha in *Jane Eyre*, they raise a host of psychological and social questions about the novel and the period in which it was written. Kelly opens by describing some established critical ideas about Gothic writing and binary oppositions. Heather, Nat, and Jason develop this as they think through specific characters in the novel in social and historical perspective. When we met face-to-face to continue the conversation, there were frequent references to what students had written in the electronic discussion. Even though these were adults and graduate students, intellectually valuable results from students exploring complex ideas and developing each other's thinking are possibilities at all levels.

Many of us require our students to read works that supplement course texts, and threaded discussions offer a marvelous way for students to share ideas about their independent reading. The posting of items can be like a series of interactive book talks, inspiring students to read titles that appeal to their classmates. For example, in one of my classes students started an item about their reading of young adult literature that generated many responses. Here are a few of their comments.

Author: Todd
11-Oct 11:32
My favorite book when I was young, and still to this day, is *Catcher in the Rye* by JD Salinger. I'm a Salinger-holic, what can I say? What attracted me to Salinger was not a teacher or a family member, but the movie *Six Degrees of Separation*. Starring a young Will Smith, the movie wasn't that good, but Smith's main character always

talked about this book called *Catcher in the Rye* and how much of an influence it was on him. I read it and now it's an influence on me.

Author: Daryth
19-Oct 10:37
I was a magic/fantasy freak when I was a kid. Yes, I would read everything I could get my hands on, but my favorites were things like C.S. Lewis's *Narnia* series, Tolkien's *Hobbit* series, a book entitled *Steel Magic* that I must have read 50,000 times, another book called *The Incredible Trip to the Mushroom Planet* and anything that had to do with your everyday kid walking into a magical situation. E. Nesbit is another favorite author (*Five Children & It, The Phoenix and the Carpet*). Looking back, I figure that these were escapist readings for me . . .

Author: Jeremy
19-Oct 11:05
My favorite series was the *Hardy Boys* series, especially the *Witchmaster's Key*. Not only was it so hard to find anywhere that I had to order it, but it was also the most intriguing of all. I think more than anything, as with most children, I liked the sense of the unknown. I also think that the *Hardy Boys* series had a lot of adult type themes written for a child to understand. As children as well as teenagers, we're always in a big hurry to grow up. We try to act and be as adult as possible. This is why our attention is grabbed by these mysteries.

Author: Janelle
22-Oct 13:05
If I were to title my life as a YA reader, I would say seriously, series, series, series! It seems like all I read when I was growing up were series of novels. For example, *The Boxcar Children, Little House on the Prairie*, and *Ramona* novels, as well as other short series' (like *Super Fudge*) by Beverly Cleary (in elementary school). Then it was all the *Anne of Green Gables* books by L.M. Montgomery, and any other little 3-book series books by her my grandma bought me; and of course what teenage girl-reader could go through Junior High without reading *Sweet Valley Twins* and *High,* and *The Babysitter's Club* series?

I have found that having some kind of book talk item in the electronic discussion in which students share their favorite reading is always a good supplement to a literature course. It creates a common culture of reading, putting students (as Nancie Atwell calls it) in the "reading zone." This particular conference item went on to a rich discussion about how English teachers can foster middle school student reading; drawing first on their own memories as middle school readers provided important inspiration. Electronic conversations that allow students to share memories and impressions and to develop their own analysis and viewpoints are likely to be engaging.

I have used electronic conferences as a support for literature circles, and the conference becomes a place where small groups of students from my classes can meet, each group in their own forum, to write and share ideas about what they are reading. (See Chapter 3 for ways of creating literature circles with blogs.) Just as Harvey Daniels has proposed, students in these groups can be assigned specific roles or activities in these discussions.

Participants Beyond the Classroom

Electronic conferencing can also invite people outside the class into the conversation—be it experts on a subject or other students from another class section or school. For example, I frequently teach more than one section of a class, and I have combined these classes into the same computer conference. Although I worried at first that some sense of intimacy might be lost since the students did not all know one another, I found that pooling students into the same computer conference actually enriched the experience. Since other students they didn't personally know were reading and responding to their ideas, they took their writing more seriously and seemed more academically focused. I have shared electronic discussion forums with class sections taught by other teachers. This required a bit more care; we found that it helped students keep activities in the online conference clear if we labeled some of the items with teacher names and others were marked "open for both classes." This approach certainly helped build connections between classes and fostered communication and community across the institution.

Case Study: Teachers

One semester I was teaching two different but related courses: an undergraduate English methods class for students preparing to be intern/student teachers, and a graduate seminar of currently practicing secondary English teachers. Combining the electronic discussion forums of these two classes had valuable results for both groups. The aspiring teachers were, of course, especially interested to hear feedback from teachers currently in the field. The surprise was the enthusiasm of the classroom teachers to participate and respond to

all of the "newbies." Several teachers, all of them teaching full loads in middle or high school, spent a good bit of time—well beyond what was required
by my class—reading and responding in detail to the undergraduates. These
practicing teachers enjoyed their well-deserved role as mentor. They wanted
to share insights and perspectives from their years of classroom experience,
and were delighted to do so with a group of aspiring teachers eager for their
wisdom.

Case Study: African Literature

An interesting experience I had joining classes in an electronic discussion forum took place when I was teaching a class in African literature, including
many great works for high school students. I had met several professors of African literature teaching in the English department at the University of Senegal in Dakar. I decided that I could incorporate into my curriculum a couple of
additional novels these African professors were teaching and that our students
would have four novels in common. (These were *Devil on the Cross, Kehinde,
So Long a Letter,* and *A Leap Out of the Dark.*) Knowing the difficulty of technology access in Africa I applied for, and was awarded, a small grant of three
hundred dollars. With this funding the African professors were able to set up
free Internet café time for their students to exchange email with my students
as "counterparts" and also to participate in our computer conference. On the
one side were my students, mainly from small towns and suburbs in western
Michigan. On the other side were kids from different tribal groups in cities and
villages in western Africa. This certainly created an opportunity to learn more
about the cultural context of the literature that my students were reading!
Clearly one of the exciting possibilities with electronic conferencing is asking
outsiders—authors, experts, community members, or other students—to join
the conversation.

While the students did discuss the literature they were reading, their
conversations soon segued to topics such as the differences between family
and daily life in Senegal and the United States. As in the novels we were
reading, many of the African students came from polygamous families and
were willing to share their experiences. While some students received email
from young Africans defending polygamy, most of the young African women
emailing my students were unambiguous about their intentions not to enter
into the same kinds of relationships as their mothers. My students in Michigan
found the conversation fascinating and were learning firsthand about tensions
and changes taking place in Africa today. Schooling and education was an-

other theme in the African literature we were reading. The college students in my class were interested in how African students attended college, what their classes were like, how they paid for school, and more. One African young man shared a story about his uncle selling a favorite mule to make it possible for them to pay his high school fees. On the other hand, my students were surprised to learn that in Africa (as in most of the world) college education is paid for mostly by the government. In short, even though the conversations were not always focused only on the literature we were reading, the exchanges were valuable to understanding cultural context.

As exciting as establishing electronic communication across continents was, there were complications. The African university semesters are scheduled very differently than ours—it was difficult to set up an exchange program that matched schedules. While over fifty African students were invited to join the Nicenet electronic conference that my students were part of, there were only a handful of students who ended up doing so, perhaps because the procedures of logging in and participating in different conference items were strange to them. (See the end of this chapter for ways to use threaded discussions with limited or no technology resources.) The exchange worked better with email than it did with the electronic conference—and this was too bad, since an electronic conference would have allowed the participants to share their communications not just between individuals but with all the members of both classes, and create an archive that future students could have looked at. Nevertheless, there were a number of rich email exchanges between the African students and my students, some that went on for months after the class was over.

One site for K–12 teachers who wish to have their students communicate electronically with groups of students in other countries is E-Pals.com, a commercial site that has fostered student-to-student email exchanges and discussion boards used in over 100,000 classrooms around the world. The site offers built-in language translators and spell checkers for many languages and costs about one dollar per student participant (in 2007 teacher accounts were thirty-nine dollars for thirty students). It has a safety function that allows the teacher to view all emails before they are sent or received. Teachers from around the world sign up and indicate where they would like to set up exchanges. This site is evidence of the amazing new opportunities for classroom-related electronic communication becoming available on the Internet. How exciting for students reading literature from another country, or from other parts of their own country, to set up an email or discussion board exchange with students from that location!

Outside the Classroom

Thinking beyond the classroom, electronic discussion boards open up many possibilities for professional collaboration. Any time that professionals or colleagues want to work together, setting up a specific threaded discussion can make that work easier and more collaborative, and it can create a record that can be referred to by others. It seems like we never have enough time to collaborate with our fellow teachers; however, a threaded discussion can make that possible, allowing teachers to participate at times that are best for them individually. For example, NCTE has set up an extensive professional development activity for language arts teachers, called "Co-Learn," utilizing online discussions. TappedIn.org is another online collaborative professional development site for public school teachers making use of threaded discussion. Although I don't have any formal relationship to former students once they are intern teaching, I have set up discussion boards so that these students, all in different schools and districts, are able to share their experiences and seek ideas from one another and me. I was able to create an electronic discussion board for faculty members at my university who were reading recent research as a group, allowing us to continue our conversations beyond meeting times and also propose and discuss ideas for selecting future readings. While working on a book about doctoral programs in English education, I invited a number of doctoral students and recent graduates from different universities to respond to questions about their experience. The edited transcript of this discussion became the first chapter of a book on doctoral programs in English education.

▪ Metacognition and Teacher Reflection

Electronic conferences facilitate metacognition, helping me reflect on what students are learning, how the class is going, and how well I am teaching. I frequently create an item for students to talk about their progress on major assignments as well as how they think the class is going. Such a conversation is useful to me as a teacher, and (in the electronic conference) one that I can participate in when I see fit. In our electronic discussions, I frequently create items where students and the teacher can reflect and exchange ideas on how to improve the course, what constitutes a good electronic discussion, and how students can develop and improve their posts. When I have special events in my classes—such as a visiting speaker, a field trip, or attendance at a poetry reading or conference—I always create a related item on the electronic conference for student reflection. The electronic conference allows students to continue discussing ideas and activities that come up in the course, sometimes long after the class has moved on to another topic.

One of the remarkable features of electronic discussions is the archive they create for self-reflection. An electronic conference can serve as a portfolio of informal student writing—I have asked students to look over their computer conference contributions for the semester and write about what they have learned or how they have grown. Student writing can also be copied and pasted into an electronic conference, creating opportunities for group feedback. Of course, looking back over a semester of student writing can lead the teacher to new insights about how to organize a class and focus discussion. When I have wanted to capture for others the nature of a classroom experience, I've published transcripts from student electronic conferencing (as I have in this book). Writing this chapter, I have gone back and reread some of the different electronic discussions that my students engaged in, some as long as fourteen years ago. Reading these conversations vividly brings back to mind particular students, conversations we had, and issues we were dealing with. I notice important differences in the tenor of their responses on certain topics. I wondered whether I've changed the way I teach or whether a time and cultural gap has changed the way we all think. In our hectic lives as teachers it is sometimes hard to find the time or the materials that will let us reflect on our own growth. If an archive of electronic conferences can make that possible then it is certainly a worthy addition.

FIGURE 2–4 *Using electronic discussions in the literature classroom*

Entering	Close Reading	Contextualizing	Responding
Create classroom community	Develop textual analysis in collaborations	Bring authors, experts, and others into the discussion	Develop ideas in writing in an informal, collaborative environment
Foster freedom of expression	Return and study student and teacher comments with time and care	Discuss ideas with students in other classes, contexts, and countries	Publish creative or analytical writing for the whole class to read and comment on
Experiment with ideas			
Hold pre-reading discussions	Cut and paste literary texts and student writing into forums		

Focused and interactive writing is the primary activity of electronic discussions and the format can clearly be used to facilitate entering into the story world of a text, closely understanding its meaning; considering its social, cultural, and political context; and developing personal and collective responses (see Figure 2–4).

■ Looking Ahead: Open-Source Course Management Systems

Electronic discussions have been around since the mid-1990s, and now come packaged with course management systems such as Blackboard. Such packages now include grade books, group work areas, digital drop boxes for student work, communication tools, chat rooms, and more. Most of these tools are available outside of the course management system, but having them packaged together is convenient, especially for teachers who are not especially Web savvy. According to the Blackboard site, it is now used by millions of students in colleges, universities, and K–12 schools around the globe. Partly owned by Microsoft, Blackboard has been aggressively trying to patent and market its products to universities and, increasingly, to secondary schools.

There are open-source alternatives to Blackboard. In addition to Nicenet (the Web-based course management system I use) I have also experimented with Moodle, a software application that it is free to schools, universities, and anyone else. Moreover, open-source software allows large numbers of people to participate in its development and improvement. This is often done by adding modifications or *mods*. Many programmers working in schools and universities are willing to develop mods to improve Moodle, and release these to others (again) for free. Mods can make the software better adapted to a particular use or situation. If many people are eagerly improving an open-source application for free, over time it becomes difficult for a traditional software company to keep up.

Moreover, there is something attractive and democratic about user modification and sharing. Even Benjamin Franklin has been identified as an "open sourcer." After profiting for a number of years, Franklin donated his inventions to the public domain—including the Franklin stove, bifocals, and the lightning rod. Wikipedia is an example of a resource created by gratuitous contributions of over 75,000 contributors. Given restrictive budgets, it is important for teachers and schools to know about open-source software. At sites such as OpenSourceWindows.org, OpenSourceMac.org, and SourceForge.net you can find free, high-quality software that can be downloaded for word processing, Web browsing, email, file sharing, photo editing, video production, podcasting, and other applications.

Electronic discussions are here to stay, whether teachers use a commercial program or avail themselves of free resources. We are living in an increasingly connected global world, and helping students learn to communicate and work with others in online environments is critical. The next chapter takes us into a variety of powerful new ways for students to elaborate, share, and deepen their thinking.

Using Electronic Discussions with Limited or No Technology Resources

As we shuttle back and forth from technology-enriched activities to traditional English teaching, we have realized that a number of the instructional strategies we have learned from computers and the Internet can, with a little imagination, work well with pen and paper. The kind of focused collaborative writing created by online discussion tools can also be replicated in a classroom with limited technology.

- In a one-computer classroom, you can use the data projector to show students how to log in and to model appropriate responses.

- You might also require students to reply to a threaded discussion topic as homework, provided that students have home or after-school access.

- In a classroom without a computer, try using notepads—headed with different questions—that students pass around the room to respond to the question and one another's comments. The notepads might also be assigned as an ongoing homework project, with notepads traveling from student to student as the unit or semester progressed. This kind of activity can take place before, during, or after a traditional face-to-face discussion. All of the writing will enhance the thoughtfulness of the spoken conversation.

Web Resources Mentioned in Chapter 2

Blackboard/WebCT (www.blackboard.com) is proprietary course management software that must be installed on a Web server. It supports course authoring, electronic discussion, chat rooms, online testing, drop box, grading, wikis, internal Web mail, rubrics, student learning data, surveys, blogs, and RSS feeds.

Desire2Learn (www.desire2learn.com) is a proprietary course management software that must be downloaded to a Web server. It supports electronic discussion, chat rooms, online testing, drop box, grading, wikis, internal Web mail, rubrics, student learning data, surveys, blogs, RSS feeds.

Epals (www.epals.com) facilitates teacher-supervised global pen pals and classroom to classroom project sharing. Over 100,000 registered classrooms.

Moodle (www.moodle.org) is a free, open source course management software system that must be downloaded to a Web server. It supports electronic discussion, chat rooms, online testing, drop box, grading, wikis, internal Web mail, instant messaging, and viewing clips from YouTube.

Nicenet (www.nicenet.org) is a free, Web-based classroom management system that includes threaded discussion, link posting, document posting, and internal email.

OpenSourceWindows.org, OpenSourceMac.org, and **Source Forge.net** are sites where free, open source software can be downloaded to Windows or Mac computers. Applications include word processing, web browsing, email, photo manipulation, audio recording, podcasting, etc.

TappedIn (www.tappedin.org) is a teacher professional development site incorporating threaded discussion, chat, discussion transcripts, open informational events.

Wikispaces (www.wikispaces.com) is a free and easy-to-use wiki that allows you to create personalized pages. For collaborative purposes, you may allow others to edit your pages, choosing between public, members only, or private access permissions. For other free wikis, see www.wetpaint.com and www.pbwiki.com.

Web 2.0: Blogs, Podcasts, and Feed Readers

3

Robert Rozema

Novelist Orson Scott Card seems to have a knack for making predictions. In his first novel, Ender's Game, *published in 1985, Card not only predicted the Internet (or "the nets," as they are called in the book), but also the influence of blogging on politics and public policy. In fact, I would argue that the character Valentine Wiggin's online persona, Demosthenes, was the very first warblogger.*

—Greg, from the Begging to Differ weblog, July 15, 2003

The main character in *Ender's Game*, the 1985 award-winning young adult novel by Orson Scott Card, is a child genius named Ender Wiggin. Ender is recruited by the military to defeat a race of aliens known as buggers, hostile extraterrestrials who nearly destroyed Earth in their previous attack years before. While Ender is being trained at battle camp through a series of strategy games that ultimately prepare him to destroy the buggers' home world, Ender's equally intelligent siblings (Valentine and Peter) attempt to gain political power on Earth by swaying public opinion about the war and its consequences. Only ten and twelve, Valentine and Peter nevertheless manage to influence the debate—and finally grasp real power—by publishing their political commentaries on what Card calls the "nets":

> "Val, *we* can say the words that everyone will be saying two weeks later. We can do that. We don't have to wait until we're grown up and safely put away in some career."
>
> "Peter, you're *twelve*."
>
> "Not on the nets I'm not. On the nets I can name myself anything I want, and so can you."
>
> . . . She had never seen him speak with such sincerity. With no hint of mockery, no trace of a lie in his voice. He was getting

better at this. Or maybe he was actually touching on the truth. "So a twelve-year-old boy and his kid sister are going to save the world?" (Card 1992, 129–32)

Though fictional, this scene may seem strangely familiar to those keeping pace with recent developments on the World Wide Web. Twelve-year-olds like Valentine and Peter are publishing their ideas to the Web—if not to save the world, then at least to keep in touch with friends, journal about their lives, respond to current events, and (if they are lucky enough) gain a readership that may number in the hundreds or even thousands. Indeed, from our perspective today, we might identify Peter and Valentine as prototypical bloggers.

A blog—short for weblog—is a sort of online journal, a website that features regularly updated, chronologically ordered posts. Beyond this most salient characteristic, blogs vary widely in purpose, format, and readership. A blog might be a personal diary read by a handful of friends, a journalistic report with enough clout to influence the mainstream media, a political soapbox, a corporate marketing tool, a commentary on other blogs, a celebrity confessional, an academic notebook, or a wartime correspondence. Most blogs allow visitors to leave comments, and the most popular blogs have thousands of visitors every day. Collectively the sum of all blogs on the Web totals over fifty million and is called the *blogosphere* (Perseus Development Corporation 2005).

The birth and explosive growth of the blogosphere is the most recognizable in a series of recent changes to the World Wide Web. Over the past few years, the Web has undergone subtle but important shifts in structure and function. Taken as a whole, these changes mark the emergence of a new Web, generally called Web 2.0. Unlike the early Web—in which expert users called webmasters developed sites with unchanging content—Web 2.0 is characterized by socially constructed and shared information, dynamic content, and easy-to-use online applications, many of them free. If the early Web gave us the online *Encyclopedia Britannica*, Web 2.0's most heralded achievement is Wikipedia, a user-created encyclopedia that anyone can edit. In other words, as *Time* proclaimed when it put a mirror on the cover of its 2007 "Person of the Year" issue, Web. 2.0 is all about you—the Web user (Grossman 2006). This chapter discusses what these changes mean for reading and responding to literature. More specifically, I look at three Web 2.0 applications that are accessible to technology novices and experts alike—weblogs, podcasts, and feed readers. And like our treatment of the other technologies, my discussion of Web 2.0 applications will show how these new tools can reinforce and extend the goals and practices of literature instruction.

Blogging in the Literature Classroom

According to a survey conducted by Perseus Development Corporation, nearly 60 percent of blogs are created by teenagers (2005). While many of these blogs are abandoned shortly after start-up, it is a fact that every day hundreds of thousands of adolescents spend time writing their personal weblogs. Often these blogs are embedded within social networking sites such as MySpace, Bebo, or Facebook, where millions of young people have created personalized pages with pictures, music, videos, links to friends, and social applications. Not unexpectedly, adolescent blogs typically focus on social issues such as dating or school life and are characterized by unconventional spellings, truncated syntax, and e-logisms that tend to drive most English teachers crazy—IMHO for *in my humble opinion*, to cite one example. Still, looking at these blogs can provide teachers with some insight into the writing and reading lives of young people, but only if we keep an open mind about them.

Keeping an open mind may mean ignoring the mainstream media, which in recent years has sometimes cast blogging—and particularly the social networking sites MySpace and Facebook—as the dark alley of the Web, a hangout for cyber-bullies, sexual predators, and angry outcasts plotting school shooting sprees. Over the past two years, I have tracked stories about MySpace using a feed reader, an application I describe later in this chapter. As you'll see, a feed reader is an online tool that collects headlines from news sources on the Web (including major newspapers like the *New York Times*) as well as from blogs, podcasts, and more. As articles about MySpace poured into my feed reader inbox, I found that nearly all of them dwelt on its potential dangers, from accounts of teens posting inappropriate images of themselves or their friends to cautionary tales about pedophiles using MySpace to snare victims. Indeed the scare over MySpace alone has prompted Congress to propose legislation barring social networking sites from public schools and libraries that receive e-Rate federal funds. If signed into law, the Delete Online Predators Act (DOPA) will effectively prevent adolescents from accessing MySpace accounts at school, but it may also shut the door on instant messaging applications, chat rooms, wikis, and other blog services since these all technically qualify as social networking sites.

How Blogs Work

I find this situation lamentable because today more and more educators are using blogs for meaningful academic purposes. These academic blogs, sometimes called *edublogs*, have become an increasingly popular tool because they require almost no expertise, very little time, and no money to create. The *New York Times* recently reported, for instance, that second graders in a Maryland school used a class blog to write about their field trip to a Native American farm. Third graders in the same district blogged about a statewide book award (Selingo 2004). Sites such as Edublogs allow teachers to set up a class blog in a matter of minutes, and there are hundreds of commercial blogging services—many offering advanced features for no cost. The rise of edublogging has also spurred the development of online support resources: the Educational Bloggers' Network, sponsored in part by the Bay Area Writing Project, helps teachers at all levels use blogs for writing and reading instruction across the disciplines. Exemplary K–16 edublogs are archived at the EdBlogger Praxis, a valuable site that also keeps track of the latest in edublog news. And there are countless blogs about edublogging—including Weblogg-ed by former high school English teacher Will Richardson; Digital Writing, Digital Teaching by English education professor Troy Hicks; and my own blog, Secondary Worlds.

Blogs are also very simple to set up and maintain. Blogging demands no familiarity with coding language or Web design software such as Frontpage or Dreamweaver, and getting started requires only an Internet connection and about ten minutes. Most commercial services like Wordpress or Blogger provide helpful wizards that guide new users through the setup process and introduce key features. Less-experienced technology users can learn from their students, who are generally willing to show novices the ropes. In short, teachers can become proficient bloggers quickly, without in-service training or specialty software. This means that instead of focusing on technical skills, teachers can start their students blogging almost immediately. Within the English language arts, a growing number of teachers and teacher educators have taken advantage of this new, easy-to-use application, using blogs to teach writing, reading, critical thinking, and more. In a recent issue of *English Journal*, for example, Greg Weiler (2003) contends that blogs encourage both individual and collaborative writing in multiple formats, including the personal journal, classroom bulletin board, and electronic portfolio. Will Richardson (2003), whose Weblogg-ed serves as a sophisticated example of the potential of edublogging, has shown how blogs can improve discussion both in and out of the classroom. And Sara Kajder et al. (2004) connect key characteristics of blogs to best practices for the English language arts classroom—economy (blog entries need to be short), archiving (blog entries are saved), multimedia (blogs can incorporate video and audio), immediacy (the most current entries are posted at the top of the blog), and active participation (the best blogs are those with frequent posts). Allen and I have seen how blogs in our literature classrooms allow students to share their creative and critical responses to literature with real audiences; to collaborate with peers in thinking and writing about literary texts; to record the meaning-making process as it happens; and to enrich literary texts with all the biographical and historical information the Web has to offer.

Blogging About Books

One way of using blogs in a literature classroom is as an alternative to the time-honored book report. In my literature methods course, I require my secondary English education students to keep book blogs. In small groups, my students choose three to four young adult novels and post occasional entries about those novels as they read them. I require my students to respond to at least six of the prompts shown in Figure 3–1. Students may invent their own prompts, as long as their entries attempt to shed light on the text and take advantage of online resources. Group members are also expected to read and comment on one another's blogs. Throughout the semester, students meet in literature circles periodically, using their blog entries to jump-start discussion in the same way that readers might use the literature circle role sheets originally developed by Harvey Daniels (2002).

One consistent and compelling result of the book journal assignment is a change in the way students perceive audience. Writing teachers know that the question of audience is fundamental—we insist that students define their voices, weigh their purposes, and temper their diction according to the needs of their readers. Admittedly this audience can be more hypothetical than real, with much student writing (particularly those literary analysis essays) destined for our eyes only. But blogging about literature gives students a chance to write for a real audience of peers, parents, teachers, and even the global Web community. As one of my students wrote, "I liked the idea that I could treat this as a journal with an audience. I put a little more thought into my entries knowing that my peers might read them." Another added that she liked "the potential to communicate with others about books"—potential that not many of our writing assignments allow, though we certainly fantasize about students having earnest, public conversations about books.

Of course, there are risks in publishing to the Web. One inconvenience faced by educational bloggers, for instance, is the proliferation of spam blogs (*splogs*) and spam comments. Spam comments show up on unprotected blogs in the same way that spam email fills an inbox. Designed to increase the search ranking of a particular site, spam comments often link to adult sites and can

FIGURE 3–1 *Book blog prompts*

Write a first-person entry in the form of a letter, journal entry, email, or voice mail that captures the voice of the character and provides insight into him or her.

Predict what will happen as the story unfolds.

Write a missing scene the writer chose not to include.

Choose a character that you identify with and explain why.

Invent a character the writer should have included.

Make a text-to-self, text-to-text, or text-to-world connection.

Write an imaginary interview of a character or the author. Be sure your questions and answers capture or reveal something new about the character or author.

Comment on the book blog of a group member.

Link to a site that you think the main character would like. In one or two paragraphs, explain your choice.

Link to a site that provides helpful background information on the text. In one or two paragraphs, explain your choice.

Link to a site that connects thematically or topically to the novel. In one or two paragraphs, explain your choice.

Link to a review of the novel and offer a brief response to the review.

Link to a site that provides biographical information on the author. In one or two paragraphs, explain how this information affects your reading.

Link to or insert an image that connects to the text and explain your choice in one or two paragraphs.

Describe your own activity as the reader of a passage of your choice. What literary moves are you making?

Pull a quotation from the text and comment on its significance.

---

be difficult to ward off. Another risk involves unwanted attention from outsiders, who might leave offensive comments on student blogs. Finally, students themselves occasionally leave inappropriate or insensitive comments on one another's blogs.

To limit these dangers, many teachers and professors make use of the password-protection option offered by some services, effectively restricting blog access to class members alone. Or they moderate all incoming comments, another effective means of prevention. Students keeping individual blogs can also moderate incoming comments. Allen and I recommend offering students online etiquette rules—or better yet, having students develop their own guidelines. And to be safe, you should obtain administrative and parental approval prior to publishing student blogs on the Web, even when the blogs are private. You should also warn students not to post their email addresses, home addresses, or telephone numbers. Such cautions should be tempered by the fact that like any website, the popularity of a blog is measured by the number of links from other sites pointing to it. The great majority of blogs never accrue enough inbound links to gain search engine attention. So you can rest assured, if not complacently, that your particular corner of the blogosphere will not attract much outside scrutiny.

In addition to providing students with a real audience of classmates, friends, and family, blogging about literary texts also allows students to collaborate in exciting new ways. In the examples shown here, two of my students exchanged creative and critical responses to the young adult novel *The Perks of Being a Wallflower* by Steven Chbosky (1999). Ryan began by writing as a friend of the main character, a reliable prompt many of us use to foster student empathy with characters.

> 4/11/2006 A Letter to Charlie . . .
> Hi Charlie,
> Sorry I haven't responded sooner, but you write so many letters that it's hard for me to keep up sometimes. Anyways, I have been thinking a lot about what you have written, and there are a couple of things that keep bothering me. I know that we haven't met, but I am still very concerned about what's happening to you. Why have you started up with the LSD again? I understand that your feelings start to choke you sometimes and that you just want to escape but getting high off of LSD is not the solution.
>
> You're so smart and capable of so much, and it hurts to hear how down you get. Do you think that you could tell your brother about the things that bother you? I know that you don't talk much, especially with him playing football in college now, but I really feel like you need to talk with someone in your family, and your mom and dad don't seem like they get it. I'd tell you to consider talking with your sister, but I think she has issues of her own that need to be sorted out.
>
> Is there something about your Aunt Helen that you're not telling me? It just seems like your writing becomes spaced out in a weird kind of way when you talk about her. I don't know, maybe I am just reading too much into it, but sometimes I get this feeling that I can't shake, like your problems run much deeper than you're willing to let on.

You always talk about participating in life, and I think that's a skill that everyone needs to improve on, myself included. However, thanks to your letters, I feel as though I have started to participate in my life more, and I thank you for that Charlie.

What does Bill have you reading now? I wish I had an English teacher like Bill. I read *The Catcher in the Rye* after you mentioned it to me and I thought it was terrific. Holden reminds me of you in a way, but I can't quite put my finger on it. Maybe it's the fact that you both have troubles but still try to find your own path in the world. It's almost midnight, and I have to catch the six o'clock bus to school because my mom needs the car tomorrow. Anyways, I am writing you back so that you don't think that I have forgotten about you.
Your friend,
R

Ryan's entry is a blend of creative and critical writing. As a creative reader, he has imagined a character, R, who exists beyond the novel, just outside the purview of the characters and events of the story. The invented R allows Ryan to connect with Charlie—R worries about Charlie's drug use, advises him on family matters, and is pleased with his friendship with Bill. The entry also shows Ryan elaborating on the story world in a creative way, as R seems to maintain an independent existence. He has read *Catcher in the Rye* on Charlie's recommendation, for instance, and must ride the bus "because [his] mom needs the car tomorrow." Making connections to characters and extending the text are two key indicators that Ryan has entered the story world of *The Perks of Being a Wallflower*—and is caught up in it.

The entry also shows that Ryan is reading the text closely, with keen attention to detail. First, readers of the novel will recognize that Ryan's choice to write a letter to Charlie is very fitting. *Perks* is an epistolary novel in which Charlie sends a series of letters to an unknown recipient. By writing a letter in response, Ryan is answering one of the text's central questions: to whom is Charlie writing? Ryan is also making inferences here, evident in his inquiry about Aunt Helen, who is eventually exposed as Charlie's molester: "Is there something about your Aunt Helen that you're not telling me? It just seems like your writing becomes spaced out in a weird kind of way when you talk about her." What is important to note is that unlike many writing assignments that ask students to analyze literature *after* reading finishes, the book blog captures meaning-making as it happens, providing teachers with more insights into the reading strategies of their students. In an earlier post on the same text, in fact,

Ryan speculated "that the story will begin to focus more on Charlie's relationship with his parents. At this point I don't feel as though Charlie's parents are very in touch with him . . ." Ryan's prediction turns out to be at least partially correct. By the end of the novel, Charlie's parents realize how Aunt Helen has abused Charlie and take measures to protect him.

Of course, paper-and-pen literary journals can foster equally rich responses, and they too can provide an ongoing record of literary meaning-making. The book blog, however, lets students collaborate in a way that is unique to the digital medium—by leaving comments or writing longer responses on their own blogs. In response to Ryan, for example, Kristi posted the following entry on her blog:

> 4/11/2006 Response to Ryan
>
> Ryan,
>
> I am intrigued by the idea that you had to write back to Charlie from the perspective of the "dear reader." First of all, I really like the fact that you discourage Charlie from using LSD, especially when his school friends aren't exactly positive role models in that aspect. Also, your entry seems very personal and attentive to what is going on in Charlie's life, which is exactly what he needed. I also like the fact that you give Charlie advice about what to do such as talking to his brother. Maybe it never occurred to him, or maybe he needed to hear it from someone else that it would be okay.
>
> I also agree that there may be something more to Charlie and Aunt Helen. Charlie does seem to drift in and out of his writing in a way that readers may sense that there is something deeper involved with what happened to Aunt Helen, and how Charlie feels about it. The issue with Aunt Helen is so apparent in his life that there must be more to the story than he lets on in his letters.
>
> Also, it is great that you wrote back to Charlie in a perspective of someone who is around as the character you created. Moreover, it is interesting that you allude to the notion of "participating in life." Charlie seems to sit back a lot of times and observe others more than he participates. Great connection to the text.

Notice that Kristi posted her response on the same day Ryan wrote his letter—just a few hours later, in fact. The blog allowed her to give feedback to Ryan almost immediately, without the inconvenience of giving him a paper copy during class. More importantly, the response shows that Ryan and Kristi are working together to figure out Aunt Helen: Kristi agrees with Ryan that "the issue with Aunt Helen is so apparent . . . that there must be more to the story than he lets on in his letters." Two other students in the group, Alicia and Crista, added their own voices to the conversation, frequently linking their entries to those written by Ryan and Kristi. In one post, for example, Crista writes that she "liked that Kristi included a new book for [Charlie] to read . . . it seems that reading books helps Charlie gain the experience of going through confusion and emerging better off, which helps him." Collectively their entries comprise a collaborative interpretation of the text, a group reading made possible by the blogging medium. Working together online also helped students discuss texts in class, as students came prepared to develop or defend their book blog entries.

Finally, the book blog assignment lets students resituate texts in historical, biographical, and sometimes critical contexts. When Jessica and her group read *The Great Gatsby*, they used Web resources to enrich and expand their responses to the text. At the beginning of her reading experience, for example, Jessica explored some online resources about the 1920s and reported on her findings in the example below. As you can see, Jessica took advantage of the Web by alerting her peers to visual and audio resources, enabling her group members to see and hear, at least in a limited way, the world of Jay Gatsby.

> 10/27/2005 *The Great Gatsby* Era
> *The Great Gatsby* takes place in the 1920s. Since none of us in this class, or our future students, were alive in the 1920s, I thought it would be a great idea to take a look at the Roaring Twenties. There are tons of websites that talk about different things that were going on during the time that *The Great Gatsby* is taking place. One really exciting site that I found is called <u>The 1920s Experience</u>. On this site you can take a look at the events that were occurring during the 1920s, along with inventions, people, art, literature, music, entertainment, and fads and fashions. Gatsby always had music playing at his parties, and this site lets you listen to a little clip of music while you read about some musicians of that time.
>
> I found another site that lists some very interesting facts about the 1920s at the Kingwood College Library. This site informed me that if I lived during Gatsby's time that it would have taken me 13 days to get to California. Another interesting fact about this time period is that the average salary was $1238 and for teachers it was $970. The clothing in the 1920s was very different from before. It was very risky for a lady to show her legs! I found a Web page that shows <u>the transitioning of hemlines from 1918 to the 1920s</u>. This page provides a lot of information about women's fashion in the

1920s. I had a really difficult time trying to find images of men's clothing from the 1920s, but I did find one image here.

I found a great article that talks about the Roaring Twenties and everything that happened during that time period at <u>Wikipedia</u>. I would use this information along with other information from different websites and books to help engage my students learning with *The Great Gatsby*. I believe providing background information on this time period is essential when reading this book.

While not as in-depth as more traditional written analysis, her post pointed to valuable resources and served as a starting point for group discussion, both in class and online. Moving beyond background information, another student in the same group examined sites dedicated to feminist critical theory and then posted a brief feminist interpretation of Daisy Buchanan. This post could be used to stimulate a longer, more intensive literary analysis essay.

When Allen used blogs with his introductory literature course, he saw many of the same results I did, and he particularly liked the way students used their blogs to share online resources. Since Allen required students to read from online poetry archives (see Chapter 1), the blog provided a wonderful means for students to comment on poems and to direct classmates to poems, poets, and poetry sites that they liked. When one student found a favorite poet, Billy Collins, the comments on his blog led several other students to read some of Collins' poetry and comment on their blogs. Another student found an archive of recorded poetry, with many of the poems read by the poets themselves. Other students followed the links on his blog to listen to recorded poems. When they found something they liked linked from a blog, students would often leave a message that could be read by the next student to visit the blog, thus creating a buzz about the literature that they were finding and reading.

Both of us believe that blogging about literature allows students to achieve the goals we outlined in the introduction of this book, providing students with a new way of entering the story world, a new tool for close critical analysis, a nearly endless resource of contextual information, and an appealing new medium for creative responses. "The blog assignment will excite students more than a 'write a paragraph about the story' assignment," wrote one of my students at the conclusion of the semester. "It will give kids the opportunity to discuss books with their peers without the awkwardness that sometimes happens in the classroom, and the entries will give me an opportunity to see whether my students are reading. . . . I just hope I have the opportunity to use blogs in my classroom." As teacher educators who have seen blogs work in their own classrooms, we encourage you to take advantage of this opportunity.

■ Podcasting

Another new technology emerging from the Web 2.0 revolution is the podcast. Simply defined, a podcast is audio delivered over the Web in serialized episodes. You might even think of a podcast as a blog in audio form: like the blogger, the podcaster publishes content to the Web on a regular basis—only in this case the content is recorded rather than written. Listening to a podcast requires free media software such as iTunes or Windows Media Player, or a feed reader such as Google Reader. Once installed, this software—sometimes called a *podcatcher*—finds, downloads, and plays podcasts. Podcasts may be transferred to a personal MP3 player for portable listening, but this is not a necessary piece of hardware. In fact, the idea that podcasting requires an iPod is a persistent misconception, perhaps because *pod* is associated with the iPod, the ubiquitous MP3 player with the trademark white earbuds and snazzy television spots. I recommend thinking of *pod* as an acronym for *personal on-demand*, a good description of the highly individualized and instantly available content that podcasts offer.

As with blogs, podcasts can take a variety of forms and can cover a wide range of subjects. Many mainstream media outlets now offer complete or supplemental programming via podcast: National Public Radio, for example, podcasts its award-winning "This I Believe" essay series; the *New York Times* offers, among others, a podcast that summarizes the major headlines of the day. Some podcasts provide alternative takes on the mainstream media. The *Alive in Baghdad* podcast, for instance, is produced by a team of Iraqi and American journalists and aims to "counter the sound-bite driven" news by recording the real stories of Iraqis living through the war. But podcasting goes well beyond mainstream topics: special interest groups use podcasts to advocate their causes, and individuals publish podcasts on pet topics. The podcasts archived at iTunes alone seem to cover nearly every subject imaginable, from Harry Potter (*Mugglecast*) to hairstyles (*Secrets of Style with Kim Foley*) to hairballs (*Purina Animal Advice Podcast Series*). And iTunes is only one of hundreds of podcast directories. Other popular sites include Podcast Alley and Podcasting News. Some podcasts are even enhanced with video, and in the ever-evolving language of the Web, these are known as *vodcasts*.

Podcasting and the English Language Arts

Teacher- and student-produced podcasts are becoming more popular at every instructional level, as educators explore the medium as a new way of teaching and learning. The Educational Podcasting Network lists hundreds of podcasts intended for a range of disciplines. A sampling from the ever-growing category of English language arts yields *Shakespeare by Another Name*, a scholarly podcast on the Shakespeare authorship debate; *Podcast Bangladesh*, a student-produced podcast featuring sixth graders from Bangladesh reciting their poetry; and *The Daily Idiom*, a guide to American English intended for second-language learners. Vibrant, entertaining, and nearly always informative, these examples illustrate just some of the potential of the podcasting genre.

This potential is most evident when students produce podcasts themselves. Like keeping a blog, publishing a podcast gives student writers a real audience, a new opportunity for purposeful writing and revision, a chance to collaborate with peers, and—unlike the fusty book report—a genre that actually exists outside of the English classroom. These attributes transfer well to the literature classroom, where students can podcast about literary works in a number of interesting ways. In my literature methods course, for example, students use free recording/editing software called Audacity to create short podcasts based on young adult novels. I tell my students to consider their podcast a book talk in audio form: its main objective is to interest adolescent readers in a particular book. And like a book talk, the podcast must include an engaging opener, key excerpts from the text, basic information about the plot, and the name of the author and title. Podcasters must also get permission for and credit any copyrighted music they use or use music licensed under a Creative Commons agreement (see Web resources at the conclusion of this chapter). Fulfilling all of these criteria in four to five minutes presents a challenge of economy for my students, who may work individually or collaboratively on the project.

During a recent semester, four of my students worked together to create a brilliant podcast on the young adult novel *Feed* by M. T. Anderson. A perennial favorite among my students, *Feed* is set in a futuristic world where everyone has a computer implant that feeds them information continuously. In the words of Titus, the teenage protagonist of the novel:

> People were really excited when they first came out with feeds. It was all *da da da, this big educational thing, da da da, your child will have the advantage, encyclopedias at their fingertips, closer than their fingertips, etc.* That's one of the great things about the feed . . . that you can be supersmart without ever working. Everyone is super-smart now. You can look things up automatic, like science and history . . . But the braggest thing about the feed, the thing that made it really big, is that it knows everything you want and hope for, sometimes before you even know what those things are . . . Everything we think and feel is taken in by the corporations . . . and they

can get to know what it is we need, so all you have to do is want something and there's a chance it will be yours. (2002, 39–40)

Feed tells the story of Titus and his friends, and what harmful effects occur when one of them, Violet, loses her feed during an ill-fated excursion to the moon. The novel is a satire of our dependence on technology, our culture of consumption, and the corruptive power of the mainstream media. As such, it is the perfect companion to *Brave New World* by Aldous Huxley and a fitting choice for a podcast.

Many podcasts are recorded off-the-cuff, but my students write scripts as part of the podcast assignment. I want students to craft their podcasts with care, paying special attention to mood, form, selection of key quotes, perspective, and audience. Below is an excerpt from the *Feed* podcast script—coauthored by Benny, Bethany, David, and Julie—exemplifying how the assignment elicited rich, text-centered student writing. Note that the italicized text is taken directly from the novel.

Characters (voices)
Titus
Announcer 1
Announcer 2
Announcer 3
Announcer 4
Policeman
Violet
Violet's father
[Music begins: medium tempo trip-hop. "The Sound" by Lunatic Calm]
0:01
Titus: What's the Feed?
I don't know when they first had feeds. Like maybe fifty or a hundred years ago. Before that, they had to use their hands and their eyes. Computers were all outside the body. They carried them around outside of them, in their hands, like if you carried your lungs in a briefcase and opened it to breathe.

You can be super-smart now without ever working. Everyone is supersmart now. You can look things up automatic, like science and history.

Everything that goes on, goes on on the feed. Feedcasts instant news . . . all the entertainment.
0:45
Titus: *. . . it knows everything you want and hope for, sometimes before you even know what those things are . . . everything we think and feel*

is taken in by the corporations and the feed . . . so all you have to do is want something, and there's a chance it will be yours—

Announcer 1: [cuts off Titus's voice]: *. . . attracted to is powerful T44 fermion lift with vertical rise of fifty feet per second—and if you like comfort, quality, and class, the supple upholstery and ergonomically designed dash will . . .* [fades off into Announcer 2]

Announcer 2: [fades in during Announcer 1] *. . . only on Sports-Vox—take a man, take a gas sled, take a chlorine storm on Jupiter, and boys it's time to spit into the wind with Alex Needtham, the hardest, hippest, hypest . . .* [fades off into Announcer 3]

Announcer 3: [fades in during Announcer 2] *. . . month's summer styles, and the word on the street is "squeaky" . . .*

1:30

Titus: *We went to the moon to have fun . . . but the moon turned out to completely suck. After your first few times there, when you get over being like, Whoa unit! The Moon! . . . instead there's just the rockiness, and the suckiness, and the craters all being full of old broken shit, like domes nobody's using anymore and wrappers and claws.*

But I met a girl unlike anyone I'd ever met before . . . She was the most beautiful girl, like, ever. She was on the moon all alone. Here it was spring break and she was on the moon, where there was all this meg action, and she was there without friends . . .

Her name was Violet.

[Music changes to rapid techno. "Two Telephone Calls and an Air Raid" by Shaun Imrei]

Even in the short excerpt here, it is evident that my students are working to capture the essence of the novel. To begin, their music selections match the mood of the story: the background tracks sound futuristic and are as hypnotic as the feed itself would be. In our attempt to teach the concept of mood, we often ask students to describe the emotional feel of a literary text, all the while knowing that the *mood* of a piece is hard to define and highly subjective. I happen to think that Frost's "The Road Not Taken," for example, might well be tongue-in-cheek; one of my students finds the opening scene of Steinbeck's *Of Mice and Men* to be darkly comic. Asking students to match music to language gives them a more concrete way to understand and talk about mood. With their nearly universal love of music, students are astute at finding the perfect musical accompaniment to a text. For example, their podcasts have matched *The A-List* by Zoey Dean with the lush melody of "Bittersweet Symphony" by The Verve; *The Sisterhood of the Traveling Pants* by Ann Brashares with the melancholic "In Your Eyes" by Peter Gabriel; and *Monster* by Walter Dean Myers with the intense beat of "Clubbed to Death" by Rob Dougan.

Another interesting literary element of the *Feed* podcast is its form. Quite perceptively, my students chose to mimic the effect of the feed by interrupting their main narrative with a barrage of advertisements for automobiles, clothing, vacations, dance clubs, and more. No doubt they drew their inspiration from the novel—M. T. Anderson repeatedly inserts feed fragments into the storyline of Titus and his friends, subjecting the reader to a textual version of the feed. The *Feed* podcast intensifies this effect by translating the feed into an audio format. As the podcast is interrupted again and again by obnoxious commercials, listeners get a sense of what living with the feed would be like. While the *Feed* group found a fitting form for their podcast, other students discovered that existing genres worked well for their texts—genres that included the radio interview, the television courtroom drama, and reality programming. As they craft their podcasts, students are generally careful to observe the conventions of these genres, particularly as they translate a visual genre to an aural genre. The podcast assignment, then, serves as one way to get students thinking about an important literary idea: genre.

At the heart of the *Feed* podcast are selections from the novel—selections that have been truncated and pieced together for maximum effect. If there is a single mantra in literature study, one phrase we repeat ad infinitum to students, it is *support your ideas with details from the text*. As every literary critic knows, this means highlighting meaningful passages and deemphasizing less important ones. The condensed format of the podcast puts the selection of excerpts at a premium. What quotations best represent characters, settings, or key moments in the plot? How might these quotations be integrated into the podcast without seeming abrupt or forced? Creating podcasts requires students to consider these questions. It also gets students thinking about the difference between dramatization and narrative summary. The *Feed* group relied on dramatization: their podcast consists almost entirely of direct quotations from the text. The risk here is that the quotations might fail to hang together and the final product might seem disjointed. A more narrative approach glues quotations together with bits of summary, but in doing so also risks losing some of its dramatic punch. Students must make the appropriate choice by looking into their texts. *Monster*, for example, is told as a screenplay and lends itself to a more dramatic approach. *The Sisterhood of the Traveling Pants*, however, has a large cast of characters and is better suited to a more narrative podcast.

Writing a podcast also involves another important literary idea: perspective. Students must decide how to talk about their texts—as outsiders to the story, as the characters themselves, or as both. The *Feed* podcast is told from a first-person perspective, with the voice of Titus retelling the story's events. The same is true of the *Monster* podcast. Others, though, employ both a third-person narrator and first-person characters. In these cases, students must indicate where the switches in perspective occur. Usually this means introducing a new voice, modifying a voice through a special audio effect, or changing the music to tell the listener that a new speaker is taking over. These audio indicators are analogous to the devices that writers use to inform readers that a change in perspective has occurred.

Finally, as in the case of all online publishing, podcasting about books gives students a real audience. My university students write their podcasts for an adolescent audience, creating short and appealing podcasts after the movie trailer model. Like movie trailers, their podcasts must begin with an engaging hook, reveal details about the plot but not say too much, and move toward a dramatic conclusion that leaves the audience wanting more. The students know that a podcast without an interesting opener will quickly lose its audience; a podcast without well-chosen excerpts and multiple voices will bore its audience; and a podcast without brisk pacing and an overall emotional impression will leave its audience flat. They write with adolescents in mind—young readers with short attention spans.

Podcasting's Educational Reach

The podcasts are also useful for students who listen to them as they search for interesting books to read. At the beginning of the semester, I play podcasts to entice my students into reading superb young adult (YA) novels such as *Feed*, *Monster*, *The Chocolate War*, and others. Listening to these podcasts also gives students a sense of the podcast assignment, which in turn shapes the way they read the novel. Over the past few years, I have accumulated over thirty student podcasts. Listening to five or six one day early in the semester, one of my students said that she "wanted to make hundreds of these for [her] own students." It would take time, but it is conceivable for a teacher to collect a rich audio archive of hundreds of student podcasts, all readily available for downloading and listening. In this way, the podcast becomes another form of text that students learn to read.

To broaden the audience even further, I publish the best student podcasts to iTunes at the end of every semester. Together these exemplary podcasts make up *YA! Cast*, which, like all podcasts at iTunes, is free to download. *YA! Cast* now has over twenty individual episodes, including the *Feed* podcast described in this chapter. The process of publishing *YA! Cast* is fairly simple. First I upload the podcasts (in MP3 format) to my blog, which supports file storage (many wikis also offer this feature). Then I use a free Web service called Studio Odeo to turn the uploaded MP3s into a single feed—a format that enables the podcast to be syndicated for subscription. There are other services similar to Studio Odeo, but few offer as many easy-to-use features. Studio Odeo provides, for example, an online recording studio that lets users create podcasts in one simple step. Once the feed is created, Studio Odeo also allows me to tag each episode of the podcast with descriptors and images that make the podcast easy to find. I tag each book podcast with its title, author, student writers, and an image of the book cover. Finally I submit the feed to iTunes, which reviews the content of the podcast for copyright violations and if the podcast passes muster, makes it available for download. Both Studio Odeo and iTunes provide more in-depth explanations of this process.

The best way to understand the potential of podcasting in literature instruction may be to listen to the podcasts described in this chapter, along with other educational podcasts available at iTunes and the Educational Podcast Network. Using the podcast as an audio book talk is just one idea. Students might also create an audio research report on an author, record a discussion of a short story, dramatize a Shakespearian scene, create a walking tour of the setting of a novel, or dozens of other possibilities. Allen's students have interviewed older people about how the media were different when they were younger and then posted their podcasts to the Web. The whole class listened to them, discussed them, and wrote about them. Allen has also interviewed students about their success in completing a group assignment; that podcast was posted on the Web to help students in future classes. His students have also podcasted about their experience as intern teachers, and their recordings have become a resource for future interns.

Students also find podcasts a rewarding experience. At the end of a podcast project, one of my students wrote the following: "A podcast would be so much more interesting compared to a boring book report. . . . Students would enjoy this sort of assignment since it involves creativity and technology. I also think podcasting could reach out to a lot of students who aren't necessarily the good students because it's giving them so many choices. They get to choose what they say about the book, what music to use, the pacing, the tone. . . . The podcast would be my number one alternative to the book report."

Reading with a Feed Reader

The final Web 2.0 technology discussed in this chapter is the feed reader (also called an RSS aggregator), a tool that reinvents the way we gather and sort information on the Web. To understand an RSS aggregator, which stands for either Rich Site Summary or Really Simple Syndication, it is useful to envision two methods of purchasing a newspaper. Using the first method, I walk to a newsstand, sort through the papers, purchase my favorite, and return home to read it. Using the second method, I subscribe to a newspaper and it arrives on my doorstep. Before the development of RSS, gathering information on the Web followed the newsstand model: we browsed to our bookmarked sites one at a time, stopping to read articles that caught our attention before moving on to the next site. Using a feed reader makes the process more akin to the subscription model: the news comes to us, arriving on our electronic doorstep, not just once per day but whenever updated information becomes available. Better yet, the feed reader allows us to choose what information we want. I use a feed reader to subscribe to the education sections from the *New York Times* and the *Washington Post*; technology stories from the BBC and *Wired*; National Public Radio's "This I Believe" podcast; Will Richardson's Weblogg-ed; all of my students' blogs, and much more. To return momentarily to *Feed*, we might say that using an RSS aggregator amounts to being on a feed of sorts, except we have control over the content and can access it whenever and wherever we like. A screenshot of Google Reader (Figure 3–2), the feed reader that I currently use, may serve to clarify how the application works.

The left vertical frame displays the subscriptions that I currently read, all of which have been organized into separate folders. Under the folder Education News, for example, the *New York Times* and the *Washington Post* are both listed. Both of these papers allow users to subscribe to individual sections, as do most major newspapers. In the right horizontal frame, the headlines from the education sections of the *Times* and the *Post* are displayed. Notice that the headlines are listed chronologically, with the most recent headlines at the top. Each time either newspaper publishes a new article in its education section, Google Reader automatically updates its content. If I am interested in reading an article that appears, I just click on the headline to access it immediately, or tag it with a star for later reading.

As you can tell from the screenshot, I also use Google Reader to subscribe to blogs and podcasts. A feed reader is very helpful for keeping tabs on student blogs, which can be bundled into a single feed for easy reading. More and more Web content is available via subscription, and hence is accessible through applications like Google Reader. Any site that features a small orange icon with RSS, XML, ATOM, or POD written on or next to it (or in place of the icon) offers syndicated content—content that a feed reader can aggregate. And Google Reader is just one of dozens and dozens of Web-based aggregators; other popular aggregators include Bloglines and NewsGator.

Subscribing to a feed is simple with any of these aggregators. With Google Reader, there are several ways to add new feeds. Google offers a few prepackaged bundles that allow you to subscribe to multiple news sources with one easy click. A slightly more labor-intensive technique is to visit a site to which you would like to subscribe (e.g., CNN or Weblogg-ed), find the RSS icon, copy the link shortcut (right-click), return to Google Reader, select *Add a Subscription*, and paste the URL into the box. You should then receive notification that you have subscribed to a feed, and the most current headlines from that source should appear in the right frame.

But subscribing to a prepackaged bundle or an individual feed is just the beginning. Imagine that you wanted *all* the current articles being written on a given topic—the controversy that MySpace is causing in schools, for instance. You can use Google Reader to collect all online articles mentioning *MySpace* and *school* and keep you posted whenever a new article appears. Begin by going to another Google site, Google News (Figure 3–3), and entering the search query *MySpace schools*. Google News archives over 4,500 newspapers,

FIGURE 3–2 *Google Reader*

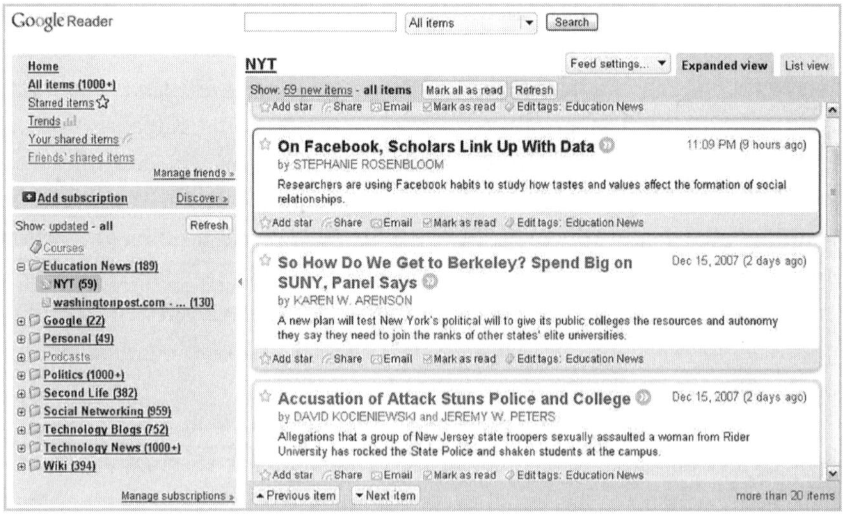

Screenshot courtesy of Google™

FIGURE 3–3 *Google News*

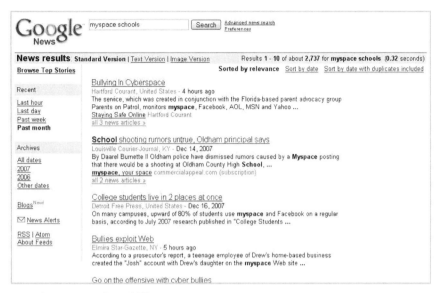

Screenshot courtesy of Google ™

so chances are your search will yield dozens of articles. You could visit each of these individually by clicking through to the article on the news site. But it's much easier to subscribe to the search query itself by right-clicking on the RSS indicator on the left sidebar and adding a new feed to your Google Reader account. Adding articles from blogs that mention *MySpace schools* is just as easy: again, just copy the *blog* link from the left sidebar and add the feed. Now you'll receive all the articles mentioning these terms, perhaps more than you ever wanted. In fact, you will soon learn to skim your inbox for relevant headlines—an important reading skill to pass along to your students.

Feed Readers in the Literature Classroom

The feed reader, then, is a useful tool for locating and sorting current information on both broad subjects (e.g., education) and smaller issues (e.g., nutrition in school cafeterias). As more and more online content is syndicated, the ability to use a feed reader to collect podcasts, news stories, blog entries, videos, and even scholarly articles will become an integral part of technology literacy. Surprisingly, though, very few teachers know about this technology: in a recent *Blogs for Learning* article, David Parry estimates that less than 10 percent of the Web users are aware of RSS. We believe that RSS technology is uniquely suited to achieve some of our most important goals as English teachers. While we are still exploring its potential applications, we think that feed readers can help us research and write about literature.

One complaint often levied by our students, for instance, is that the books we teach—*Lord of the Flies*, *To Kill a Mockingbird*, *Things Fall Apart*, *The Way to Rainy Mountain*—just don't seem relevant to contemporary life. We are stung all too frequently by the question, "How am I going to use this in real life?" because we value literary truth and beauty on their own merit and not for their ability to increase our market value or help us climb the corporate ladder. Still, if we are to make literature (and particularly the classics) accessible, we are obligated to make tangible connections to our students' lives. Feed readers can help us meet this obligation. Imagine, for example, drawing thematic parallels between *Lord of the Flies* and contemporary issues. Students could use feed readers to collect news stories on violence in schools, for instance, comparing current cases of youth aggression to the deadly misbehavior of Ralph, Jack, and the rest of the *Lord of the Flies* gang. *To Kill a Mockingbird* raises so many issues that might be addressed through a contemporary lens: race relations, the treatment of the mentally ill, and education, to name just three. A feed reader can also help us enrich students' understanding of literary texts from other cultures. Supplementing *Things Fall Apart* with news articles covering current events in Nigeria could illustrate the lasting impact of British imperialism on the Igbo culture; aggregating articles about Native Americans could help readers understand the Kiowa history and culture depicted in *The Way to Rainy Mountain*.

In a young adult context, feed readers could gather information on a host of issues central to many YA novels. Although the term "problem novel" is sometimes disparagingly attached to such works, the fact remains that many young adult texts explore social issues that are very real to adolescents, including sexual maturation, substance abuse, divorce, body image, depression, and others. In the case of *Perks of Being a Wallflower*, for example, a student might use Google Reader to find articles on teenage sexuality, child abuse, and suicide, connecting these articles to the experiences of Charlie and other characters in the novel.

Making these connections might involve students keeping an academic blog—essentially, a weblog informed by articles gathered by a feed reader. Maintaining an academic blog requires students to use Google Reader or another aggregator to locate relevant articles on a given topic. Then they respond to these articles on their blogs, using key quotations to support their ideas, citing the article, and linking to its original source. In my literature methods course, students keep academic blogs about issues related to English education.

Some of these students choose to blog about the social issues raised by the YA novels they are reading; others choose less literary but equally relevant topics, such as No Child Left Behind, censorship, or urban education. For more on academic blogging, see Chapter 5.

No doubt you will discover even more meaningful ways of using feed readers in the context of literature instruction (see the end of this chapter for ways of using feed readers, podcasts, and blogs with limited or no technology). If you believe, as we do, that literature addresses ongoing human concerns—that *The Tempest* is as powerful in a post–September 11 world as it was in Shakespeare's England—then we recommend the feed reader as an effective new way of staying current and connecting the world in which we live to the worlds of the texts we teach.

I began this chapter by suggesting that the arrival of 2.0 technologies offers English teachers new ways to achieve our goals. Reflecting again on the four key goals of literature instruction that Allen and I identified in the introduction—entering the story world, close reading, contextualizing the text, and responding to the text—I will suggest that the Web 2.0 technologies described in this chapter can be used in the ways given in Figure 3–4. This list

FIGURE 3–4 *Using blogs, podcasts, and feed readers in the literature classroom*

Entering	Close Reading	Contextualizing	Responding
Blog Find images of settings or characters	**Blog** Select and respond to important quotes from the text	**Blog** Enrich text with cultural, historical, or biographical resources	**Blog** Write from the perspective of a character
Exchange literary letters with classmates	Compare and contrast translations of the text	Examine text through a critical theory lens	Discuss themes with other readers
Podcast Listen to book talk podcasts	**Podcast** Discuss and write with literary elements: mood, genre, perspective, pacing, and audience	**Podcast** Create an audio research report on the author or setting	**Podcast** Record literature circle conversation
Feed Reader Research related subjects before reading		**Feed Reader** Research related subjects during and after reading	**Feed Reader** Read and respond to online reviews of the text

is not meant to be complete, but I hope it illustrates the great potential offered by these technologies.

■ Looking Ahead: More Web 2.0 Applications

The Web 2.0 applications I have discussed here are just the beginning. One notable omission is the wiki, a powerful collaborative writing platform most famously manifested in Wikipedia, the enormous online encyclopedia written and edited, for the most part, by ordinary Web users. Allen's graduate students have experimented with this application with interesting results: using a free wiki called Wikispaces, one student devised an entire world modeled after J. R. R. Tolkien's Middle Earth, complete with place names, maps, histories, characters, and drawings. My students have written collaborative reviews of YA novels using the free Wikispaces service.

Both Allen and I have also seen pre-service and in-service teachers use MySpace and Facebook in literary ways. One idea is for students to create profiles for the characters of a novel or play. This involves writing a personal description for the character, finding a fitting image to represent him, choosing his friends, listing his favorite hobbies and music, leaving notes on other characters' pages, and blogging from his perspective—all of which are easy to accomplish on social networking sites. Students can even use social networks to indicate more complex relationships: one feature allows users to exchange private messages, so that students assuming the roles of Lady Macbeth and Macbeth could secretly conspire against Duncan, while the old king remained blissfully unaware—dramatic irony in cyberspace. If MySpace or Facebook is just too controversial, sites such as Ning allow you to build private social networks for free.

As Web 2.0 applications continue to evolve, more possibilities for the literature classroom will emerge. I have not discussed online word processors such as Google Documents, which (in addition to facilitating collaborative writing) could also eliminate the need for schools to invest in software-based word-processing programs such as Microsoft Word. My discussion has not included social bookmarking services, such as Furl and del.icio.us, which allow users to organize online resources in more democratic, more collaborative, and more useful ways. Missing here too is an examination of Flickr, the photo sharing site that lets photographers across the world share their work; Comicvine, where graphic novel fans can create and share their own superheroes; and YouTube, the site that now hosts hundreds of thousands of amateur videos. In the right hands, all of these Web 2.0 applications can be powerful tools for the teaching and learning of literature. I hope this chapter has given you a few ideas to start with. Once you do get started, I believe—in true 2.0 spirit—that the rest is up to you.

Using Blogs, Podcasts, and Feed Readers with Limited or No Technology Resources

Blogs

- With a single computer and a data projector, you can examine blogs with your students, asking them to write down the main characteristics of the exemplary blogs you view together. Your students might also make a list of undesirable characteristics by looking at a few poor examples. Once they have understood the genre and your specific requirements, students can take turns posting on a class blog by using the comment feature or a common login.

- Create paper blogs for students, with an area for the main text and an area for comments. Students can post these to a classroom bulletin board for others to comment on, or revisit them later to comment on their own entries.

Podcasts

- In a one-computer classroom, you could use the data projector to illustrate where to find podcasts and how to download them. The class as a whole could listen to a few examples, with students writing and talking about how different podcasts seem to work or not.

- The computer can also become the hub of a production center, one station in the larger process of podcast production. Using Studio Odeo, a Web-based podcast application that requires only a microphone and an Internet connection, students could take turns recording podcasts individually or in groups, while classmates worked on their own scripts.

- Even without a computer, students could still write podcast scripts: the podcast genre has defining features (e.g., intro music) that could be beneficial for students to imitate. In this case you might download podcasts from a home or library computer, burn them onto a CD, and play them for students in class—giving them a sense of the genre and a little motivation.

Feed Readers

- In a one-computer classroom, illustrate how feed readers work with a data projector. Then your students might collectively decide which feeds the class aggregator should subscribe to, perhaps making choices based on what the class is currently reading. A class studying Henrik Ibsen's *A Doll's House*, for instance, might choose to aggregate articles dealing with issues that are important to contemporary feminists such as reproductive rights, gender roles, and the workplace. At the beginning of each class, students could respond in writing to a single article of their choice.

- In the absence of any computer, you could take in a few local newspapers and ask students to find articles that deal with the same issues. As they examined sports sections, feature articles, and news stories, the class would collectively aggregate information and learn an important lesson about the pervasiveness of gender inequality.

Web Resources Mentioned in Chapter 3

Blogging and Social Networking Resources

Edblogger Praxis (www.educational.blogs.com) links to hundreds of examples of educational blogs in a range of disciplines and grade levels. To get a sense of how teachers are already using blogs, you might begin here.

Edublogs (www.edublogs.org) allows teachers to create multi-user blogs with a few easy clicks and provides a helpful support forum for members. Teachers interested in creating a single blog for all of their class members might start here.

Educational Bloggers' Network (www.ebn.weblogger.com) is a community of teachers and organizations who are dedicated to using blogs at every level of education. Sponsored in part by the Bay Area Writing Project, the network aims to help members use blogs to teach writing and reading across all subject areas.

MySpace (www.myspace.com) is the largest social networking site on the Web, with over 100 million registered users as of early 2008. Extraordinarily popular among adolescents, MySpace allows users to create profiles, keep blogs, publish images, upload music, create lists of friends, participate in forums, and more. Now banned in most schools, MySpace is frequently characterized by the media as a dangerous place for teenagers. Thanks to the popularity of MySpace, however, social networking is being put to new uses. The 2008 presidential campaign of Barack Obama, for example, made use of social networking to organize supporters.

Ning (www.ning.com) is a free service that lets you create private or public social networks.

Secondary Worlds (www.secondaryworlds.com) is Robert Rozema's blog, which he uses as a teaching tool in his English education methods courses at Grand Valley State University. See Chapter 5 for more details.

Wordpress is a free blogging application that may be installed on a school server (www.wordpress.org) or hosted by Wordpress (www.wordpress .com). Of the thousands of commercial blogging services, Wordpress is among the best, providing hundreds of professional themes, no advertisements, and many helpful features such as password protection and content syndication.

Podcasting Resources

Audacity (http://audacity.sourceforge.net) is free recording/editing software for podcasting and more. It runs on Macs and PCs, is simple to use, and offers features that are generally available only in higher-end commercial programs.

Creative Commons (www.creativecommons.org) provides an easy way for creators of original content to share their work with less restrictive copyright rules. For podcasting, the following sites offer free music under the Creative Commons license: Jamendo (www.jamendo.com), Magnatune (www.magnatune.com), Dmusic (www.dmusic.com), and Podsafe Audio (www.podsafeaudio.com).

The Educational Podcast Network (www.epnweb.org) is a directory of podcasts produced by K–16 educators and students. Podcasts are categorized according to age level and subject matter.

iTunes (www.apple.com/itunes) is free digital media software that runs on both Macs and PCs. iTunes lets users organize their media and download songs, videos, and podcasts from the iTunes store. Podcasts listed at iTunes are all free, and users may submit their own podcasts to the store.

iTunes is currently the largest podcast directory on the Web. For media on the go, iTunes also interfaces with the iPod portable media player, but you do not need an iPod to run iTunes on your computer.

Podcast Alley (www.podcastalley.com) and Podcasting News (www. podcastingnews.com) are podcast directories that list, categorize, and rank user-submitted podcasts. All include educational podcasts, though these directories also include adult content.

Studio Odeo (http://studio.odeo.com) is a simple Web-based application that lets you record podcasts, syndicate them, and add them to the Odeo directory. No special software is required.

Feed Reader Resources

Bloglines (www.bloglines.com) and **Newsgator** (www.newsgator.com) are two Web-based RSS aggregators that make subscribing to syndicated content very easy.

Google News (www.news.google.com) is a searchable database of news articles from over 4,500 online newspapers. Highly customizable, Google News lets you subscribe to search queries via Google Reader (or another RSS aggregator), enabling you to receive updated headlines on topics of your choice.

Google Reader (www.reader.google.com) is a free, Web-based RSS aggregator. Like all things Google, Google Reader has a clean design and is simple to use. Google Reader requires a Google account, which is also free. Google Reader is even more powerful when used in conjunction with Google News.

Other Web 2.0 Applications

Comic Vine (www.comic.vine.com) is social networking for superheroes. Users create customized profiles for their invented heroes, add friends or enemies, review other heroes, and peruse the growing encyclopedia of comic book lore.

Flickr (www.flickr.com) is a free photo-sharing service that allows you to upload, tag, and share your images with others.

Furl (www.furl.net) and **del.icio.us** (http://del.icio.us) are two free social bookmarking sites that keep track of your favorite places on the Web. In addition to allowing you to access your bookmarks from any computer with a Web connection, both of these services let you tag bookmarks and search other users' bookmarks for similar resources.

Google Documents (www.docs.google.com) is a Web-based word processor and spreadsheet application that allows you to upload, edit, and share documents from any computer with a Web connection.

Wikispaces (www.wikispaces.com) is a free and easy-to-use wiki that allows you to create personalized pages and offers ad-free space for K–12 educators. For collaborative purposes, you may allow others to edit your pages—choosing between public, members only, or private access permissions. For other free wikis, see www.wetpaint.com and www.pbwiki.com.

4 | Virtual Realities: Exploring Literary Worlds on the Web

Robert Rozema

> *The boundary between the inner and outer world breaks down, and the literary work of art, as so often remarked, leads us into a new world.*
>
> —Louis Rosenblatt, *The Reader, the Text, the Poem* (1978)

In the opening chapter of George Orwell's dystopian classic *1984*, protagonist Winston Smith has an unsettling encounter with O'Brien, a high-ranking member of the ruling Party. During the Two Minutes Hate, a daily propaganda session designed to reinforce Party loyalty, O'Brien catches Winston's eye. For a fraction of a second, the two make contact, leading Winston to believe that O'Brien, despite his position within the Party, may share his subversive views:

> An unmistakable message had passed. It was as though their two minds had opened and the thoughts were flowing from one into the other through their eyes. "I am with you," O'Brien seemed to be saying to him. "I know precisely what you are feeling. I know all about your contempt, your hatred, your disgust. But don't worry, I am on your side!" (1950, 18)

Readers of the novel know that O'Brien, like many of the characters who populate Orwell's nightmarish world, is not to be trusted: indeed, he has laid a subtle trap that closes on Winston as the novel unfolds. Formerly protected by his own paranoia, Winston fails to distinguish between political friends and foes. O'Brien's seemingly sympathetic glance lures him into further unorthodoxy, captivity and torture, and, finally, self-annihilation.

The atmosphere of mistrust that pervades *1984* is hardly what literature teachers strive to establish in their classrooms, yet this is exactly the
atmosphere Anne LaGrand hoped her tenth-grade honors students would
experience as they read *1984*: the suspicion and fear bred by an oppressive
totalitarian regime. Short of installing telescreens in her rural Midwestern
high school, Anne and her fifty students opted to play *Thoughtcrime*, an ex-
perimental literary simulation I developed in 2004 as part of the NCTE *1984* +
20 project.

■ Playing *1984*: You Too Can Be a Thoughtcriminal

Thoughtcrime is an online role-playing game that attempts to bring *1984* to
life. The game is one of the many literary simulations hosted within Literary Worlds, created in 2006 at Western Michigan University. The Literary
Worlds project involved building a series of simulations about canonical and
contemporary literature in an enCore MOO environment, one type of *virtual
reality* application. By *virtual reality*, I mean an immersive and participatory
world that is rendered digitally over the Web. Included in this deliberately
broad definition are single-player video games with multiplayer components
such as *Halo* or *Halflife*, MMORPG games such as *EverQuest* and *World of
Warcraft*, and MUVE environments such as *Second Life* and *There*. For the re-
mainder of this chapter, I will drop the sometimes confusing acronyms MOO
(Multi-User Object Oriented), MMORPG (Massively Multiplayer Online Role-
Playing Game), and MUVE (Multi-User Virtual Environment) in favor of the
broader term used to categorize all of these types of environments, virtual
realities.

An enCore environment might be thought of as a series of connected chat
rooms. Each user has a login and password and can talk to other players simply
by typing. Unlike a chat room, however, an enCore environment has a permanent architecture, with multiple interconnected rooms that players can explore
and (in some cases) create. The enCore platform splits the screen into two large
panels (see Figure 4–1). The left side of the screen is used for chatting—room
descriptions and events are displayed here in text. The right side of the screen,
however, looks and functions like a Web browser. It may include graphics,
icons, audio, and streaming video that correspond to the textual description
of a room, making the virtual space easier to navigate and more visually compelling than text alone. In this environment, students can take on the role of
characters and participate in events related to the literary work, including role-
plays, museum visits, and interactive games such as *Thoughtcrime*.

FIGURE 4–1 Thoughtcrime *in an enCore environment*

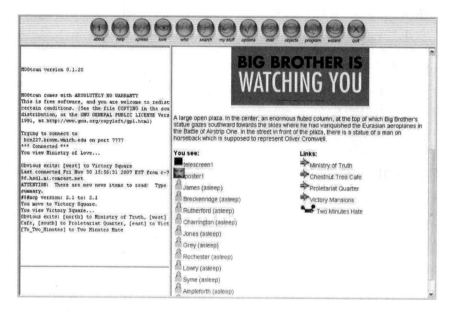

Thoughtcrime *in Practice*

In *Thoughtcrime*, students are given roles as Thought Police, Brotherhood, and Party Members. Just as in the novel, each group of characters has its own objective. Members of the Thought Police must expose and eliminate the underground revolution known as the Brotherhood; the Brotherhood, in turn, must recruit new members for their movement in the hopes of toppling Big Brother. Party Members make up the majority of the participants and face the same dilemma as Winston Smith: to join the revolution and risk death, or to attempt to guarantee their survival by betraying suspected thought criminals. The game finishes when one of the character classes achieves its objective. Sometimes this happens after only an hour or two of play, and sometimes the game lasts for a week or more. Students can get a great deal out of the activity by participating for one or two hours in a computer lab or by playing *Thoughtcrime* from their own computers as homework.

As they move through the game space—a combination of text and images that replicates key locations from the novel—students engage in furtive conversations, probing one another for information, making alliances, or, like O'Brien, giving false assurances. To help players achieve their objectives, the game gives each character class special commands (such as *vaporize*, *recruit*, or *betray*) as well as tools drawn from the lexicon of the novel (including *telescreens*, *memory holes*, and *notes*). A student role-playing as a member of the Thought Police, for example, can type *vaporize Smith* to eliminate the student playing Winston Smith; he may also type *monitor telescreen* to eavesdrop on conversations occurring in rooms with telescreens. A member of the Brotherhood, in turn, can type *recruit Smith* to add him to the ranks of the rebellion, and can type *write note* to author a secret communiqué—much like the note surreptitiously delivered into Winston's hands in the early pages of the novel. And finally, Party Members can *betray* members of the Brotherhood to ally themselves with the Thought Police. All players are unaware of one another's allegiances, and this makes up the drama of the game.

When Anne LaGrand and her honors students played *Thoughtcrime* in the spring of 2005, the game lasted for about one week. Much of the gameplay occurred in school, as Anne blended discussion of the text with periods of immersion in the online role-play; but it also occurred at home, with students logging on late in the evening to plot strategy and snare enemies. Throughout the gameplay, students wrote about their experiences in a threaded discussion that Anne created at Nicenet (see Chapter 2). One voiced what became a common theme—that *Thoughtcrime* was enjoyable: "This is so much fun . . . I want to play next year too," then added drolly, "or maybe I have no life."

Beyond being engaging, *Thoughtcrime* was designed to help students *get into* the novel—almost literally. *Thoughtcrime* introduced the dystopian setting of the novel by allowing students to explore virtual representations of its key locations; acquainted students with specific ideas and language of the novel, including *thoughtcrime*, *telescreen*, *Big Brother*, *proletariat*, and *newspeak*; and helped students connect to characters by role-playing as Party Members, Thought Police, or members of the Brotherhood. Emulating the appeal of video games popular with many adolescents, *Thoughtcrime* draws students into literature through thoughtful interaction and gameplay in a world paralleling the novel.

Logs of gameplay, along with student entries on Nicenet, illustrate that players were indeed *into* the novel, identifying with its characters and experiencing the fear and suspicion of living under a totalitarian government, at least on some level. In the following exchange, excerpted from a conversation in the Ministry of Truth Canteen, the players Hoover and Archer try to appear as orthodox as possible, as do all right-thinking citizens of Oceania. They even refuse to help Ogilvy, another player, in his attempt to "figure out who anyone is."

Archer says, "Hello Comrades."

Ogilvy says, "Hello again."

Hoover says, "HELLO."

Hoover says, "WELL THERE HAS BEEN A LOT OF VAPORIZA-TION EH?"

Ogilvy says, "Yes that is what I hear."

Archer says, "Yes serves them all right Unloyal Pukes!"

Ogilvy says, "Pukes?"

Hoover says, "THOSE WHO GET IT DESERVE IT THAT'S MY MOTTO."

Archer says, "Pukes!"

Archer says, "I concur comrade."

Ogilvy says, "Well yeah . . . but some people want to get vaporized."

Hoover says, "CONCUR DEAR ARCHER CONCUR."

Archer says, "Yes comrade."

Ogilvy says, "I don't see how anyone can figure out who any-one is."

Archer says, "It's rather easy comrade."

Hoover says, "WELL IT DOESN'T MATTER AS LONG AS THEY GET THE BAD GUYS."

Ogilvy says, "I don't understand . . . will you help me Archer?"

Hoover says, "ARCHER LET'S GO TO THE CANTEEN."

Archer says, "Sorry Comrade . . . You have to look out for yourself."

In this instance, it is clear that role-playing has engaged the players in the world of the text: Archer's caveat to Ogilvy—"look out for yourself"—and his adoption of "comrade" as a salutation show strong identification with the characters and their situations. To protect themselves, both Hoover and Archer have aligned themselves with the ruling Party, transferring their own fear and distrust onto the "unloyal pukes" who "deserve vaporization" in a manner that evokes the daily Two Minutes Hate of the novel. Many of Anne's students seemed to experience similar connections between their role-playing lives and the lives of characters in the novel. Some articulated these connections in explicit ways at the conclusion of the game:

> Playing *Thoughtcrime* is a very interesting experience. It helps you
> relate to the characters in the book and see how it might really have
> been to live in *1984*. It makes the book more fun to read.
>
> —Sheryl

I think the game is very helpful in understanding how the people in the book feel. It is fun to pretend to be a different character. It puts you into the story a little more and lets you have sympathy for the characters.

—Megan

The game has influenced my reading of the book in the fact that I can now see how difficult it is to identify the Thought Police. I have also learned how difficult it would be to meet with Brotherhood members.

—Joseph

Anne and her students' game of *Thoughtcrime* ended when the Thought Police tracked down and eliminated the six members of the Brotherhood, perhaps by imitating O'Brien's devious flattery or by monitoring late-night conversations with telescreens. In any case, the unorthodox were stamped out in a denouement that paralleled the novel's dark conclusion. After the game finished, players offered suggestions for its improvement. Many of these recommended making even stronger ties between reading the novel and playing the game. Students wanted to be able to rectify a document as Winston did for the Ministry of Truth, for example, or actually view the Two Minutes Hate video that the characters in the novel see. Besides supplying a helpful critique, such suggestions illustrate that students draw natural connections between reading fiction and *playing* fiction—connections that literature teachers can capitalize on.

Literary Worlds, Virtual Worlds

Some video game developers have already made similar connections, striving in recent years to make their games more like stories. In creating the popular *Halflife* (1998) and *Halflife 2* (2004) titles, for example, designer Marc Laidlaw wanted "to take the idea of storytelling over to a straightforward first-person shooter [game] and see how far we could get with that" (Grossman 2005, 57). Writing the characters who occupy the games, Laidlaw said, involves trying to "convey their sense of humor, their fears and vulnerabilities, and create a sense that they have an interior life and an existence that continues when they're offscreen" (Bowen 2003). But despite the literary aspirations of Laidlaw, the idea that anything resembling gaming might be used to teach literary works and concepts remains largely unexplored. Against the conventional wisdom blaming video games for a perceived decline in youth literacy, literature teachers have only begun to experiment and research the way games and more broadly virtual realities might be used to support and enhance literary reading.

Consider the similarities between literary texts and virtual realities. The appeal of literature has always been about the ability of the writer to create a believable world and of the reader to enter into that world imaginatively—to see the setting, to overhear the voices and thoughts of characters, and to anticipate and savor the events of the plot. To put it simply: learning to read literature well means learning to participate in a virtual space as if it were real. On the most basic level, virtual realities replicate this experience. Like a literary text, a virtual reality has a setting, characters, a plot, and themes. In the best video games, for example, the plot is compelling and open-ended, as in the now-classic *Jedi Knight: Dark Forces II* (1998) in which the player may follow either the light or the dark side of the force to achieve his mission. Character development is the primary goal of virtual worlds such as *Second Life* (2003) and *There* (2005). In these simulations, sometimes called *metaverses* in homage to Neil Stephenson's *Snow Crash* (1992), most players spend their time constructing virtual identities by interacting with other players and by acquiring virtual goods. Setting is crucial to massively multiplayer games like *EverQuest* (1999), which depend on realistic depictions of fantasy landscapes, usually rendered in stunning and exquisite detail. Such games may not amount to *Sense and Sensibility*, of course, but for English teachers interested in engaging teenagers—81 percent of whom play online video games (Lenhart, Madden, and Hitlin 2005)—they offer a starting place.

But where do we go from here? One possible destination suggested by Anne LaGrand's story is the enCore platform, a highly adaptable environment designed specifically for educators. The open-source enCore program is free to download, though some technical expertise is required to install it on a Web server. Once installed, it becomes a highly functional learning space. With a little practice, teachers can create virtual classrooms with desks and tables, a recorder that logs conversation, a projector that displays Web slide shows, and a VCR that plays transcripts of lectures or study guides. Dozens of higher education institutions use enCore as an educational tool within the humanities, including the University of Texas at Dallas (Lingua MOO), Texas Technical University (Texas Tech MOO), and Western Michigan University (Literary Worlds MOO). Many of these institutions are eager to host secondary teachers and their students. Literary Worlds features, for example, free online virtual activities for a variety of literary works including *Of Mice and Men, A Midsummer Night's Dream, Things Fall Apart, Native Son, The Great Gatsby, Moll*

Flanders, and *Mrs. Dalloway,* among others (see the Web resources at the end of this chapter for a complete listing).

I have found enCore to be an effective tool for creating literary simulations. Such simulations may replicate the setting of a literary work using text and static images, allow users to expand and elaborate on that setting, encourage character-based or plot-driven role-playing, host a virtual museum featuring historical or biographical information related to the text, or provide a classroom space for critical discussion of a literary work. *Thoughtcrime* is just one of many literary simulations hosted within Literary Worlds. It is also home to a *Brave New World* simulation, a multiplayer role-play I designed for my high school senior literature class in 2001. Its story further illustrates the possibilities of the enCore platform.

◼ The *Brave New World* Experiment

Building the Characters

When I taught *Brave New World* to my senior literature class, I often struggled to make the novel relevant to student lives. Some students enjoyed it immediately, but others found its futuristic setting of rigid class structures, government-sponsored drug addiction, and sexual libertinism implausible. I wanted my students to engage *Brave New World* in the way that Jeff Wilhelm describes in *You Gotta BE the Book* (1997)—to enter the story world, to visualize its setting, and to relate to its characters. For this to happen, the *Brave New World* simulation had to represent the world of the novel as closely as possible. To begin, I divided my students into the five social castes of Huxley's dystopian World State: Alphas, Betas, Gammas, Deltas, or Epsilons. In these roles, players would face caste prejudice, with some rooms programmed to be off-limits to the lower castes, and also be subjected to World State propaganda of the kind Huxley describes, as the simulation flashed hypnopaedic phrases like "Ending is better than mending," "Everyone belongs to everyone else," and "A gram is better than a damn" across the screen.

Next using just a few simple commands, I created and connected over twenty rooms, in some cases relying on Huxley's own words. As in most science fiction and fantasy, setting is crucial to *Brave New World.* Huxley spends the first three chapters of *Brave New World* detailing the strange world of his satiric imagination, delaying the introduction of the main characters until his setting is well established. This rich description made it easy for me to reproduce a virtual *Brave New World* in the simulation. To encourage my students to recognize that literary reading can involve an active and deliberate entrance into a secondary world, I designed the simulation so players would start off in the Main Lobby of the London Center of Hatchery and Conditioning, the opening location of the novel itself. Logging in, players saw this textual description:

> Main Lobby
>
> Welcome to *Brave New World*. You are in the main lobby of the London Center for Hatchery and Conditioning. The room is large and industrial looking, with polished green marble floors and stark white walls. Sitting at a large metallic desk in the center of the room is a Beta-minus receptionist. There is also a large bulletin board on the east wall. Exits include an elevator to the west and a hallway to the east. To the south, you see an indoor bumble-puppy court.

Once they entered the simulation, players were eager to explore the landscape of *Brave New World*. They moved between the Main Lobby, the Hallway, the Fertilizing Room, the Bottling Room, the Staircase, the Embryo Room, the Lift, the Dormitory, the Roof, the Hangars, and other rooms I designed. As they navigated the world of the novel, players formed mental images of its key locations. As Wilhelm suggests, making these images is essential to the reading act. Readers who successfully visualize a story world experience it as "an intense and comprehensive reality"; those who have difficulty creating images are "unable to respond in any of the other response dimensions" (1997, 56).

I hoped the simulation might encourage my students to explore the text in other ways. They might read the description of the Main Lobby and ask, "What is a Beta-minus receptionist?" or "Why am I a Delta?" More astute students might even notice the connotation of the word *hatchery* and begin to speculate on the nature of society in *Brave New World*. The simulation also provided a virtual version of soma, the recreational drug of the World State, so students could begin to understand its control over the population. Some were eager to try it, while others were more hesitant: "In which case are we supposed to get soma?" asked Gamma4 in one recorded conversation. "Don't give in to soma—resist the system!" warned Delta3 in response. Gamma4 should have heeded the caveat: taking too much virtual soma paralyzed players for five minutes.

Like *Thoughtcrime*, the *Brave New World* simulation also encouraged students to identify with characters. I required my students to create and role-play as characters who might have existed in the futuristic World State. At the beginning of the project, each student was given a generic character named according to its caste (e.g., Gamma1). After students had read the first three chapters of *Brave New World*, I asked them to individualize their characters according to the parameters of the novel. This involved choosing an appropriate character name and writing a fitting description. Since Huxley had satirical aims in naming his characters—Marx, Hoover, Ford, and Lenin all appear in the novel—I wanted students to capture the same spirit. They researched politicians, psychologists, industrialists, and scientists from Huxley's own time whom Huxley might have chosen to satirize. Students named their characters and then described their physical appearance, caste, occupation, and hobbies. The results were characters—such as the following three created by Michael, Andy, and Christopher—who might have lived in the World State alongside Bernard Marx and Lenina Crowne:

> Iven Skinner (an Alpha)
> Iven is a tall, handsome man who is head of the World State Island Management Program. He towers over you with his powerful presence and chiseled stature. As you gaze into his mysterious eyes, you see the incredible depth of his knowledge and wisdom.

> Wilbur (an Alpha)
> An Alpha Plus who looks like he knows everything about everything. (He does, actually.) Wilbur currently works as an aircraft engineer and test pilot for his privately owned aircraft manufacturing corporation. He is fairly tall for an Alpha and obviously very, very strong. Wow!

> Tito Hoover (a Delta)
> A short man, but strong in stature. Proud owner of his DDC card (Distinct Deltas Club), Tito prides himself in his khaki color clothes and his vast collection of soma bottles from all over the World State. Tito works hard at being the best Delta helicopter pusher and it shows. He's received seven awards for Best Helicopter Pusher in his union, the Delta Devils.

Outside of the simulation, these characters became reference points for class discussions. As the class progressed through the novel, students imagined where their characters were and what they were doing, with their virtual characters lending them new perspectives on the events of the novel. At the end of Chapter 4, for example, the protagonist Bernard Marx suspects that he and another character, Helmholtz Watson, are being overheard as they discuss a potentially subversive subject. Students journaled about what their simulation characters might do in this situation. Many students seemed to enjoy making imaginative leaps from the virtual world to the literary text. At the end of the semester, one student wrote that she "liked the role-playing and virtual reality aspect of it, just because it was fun to pretend and be imaginative." Or more succinctly, in the words of another student, "It was fun to live the book!"

Building the Landscape

This sort of role-playing did have its limits, however. After the initial excitement of exploring the simulation, some of my students had trouble acting in character or were unsure what to do, perhaps because unlike *Thoughtcrime*, the *Brave New World* simulation did not assign characters specific agendas. While wandering through rooms did allow students to enter the story world, visualize the setting, and identify with characters, I wanted to invite them even deeper into the story world. So I asked them to create a part of that world by constructing a building that *might have existed* in the World State.

A more sophisticated task than creating a character, this assignment required students to think deeply and carefully about the world that Huxley creates, to master the commands necessary to build and connect their buildings, to write imaginatively, and to think critically about the way Huxley uses setting as the central vehicle of his satire. Students were allowed to recreate buildings that were mentioned but not described at length in the text, but nearly all chose to design original buildings that could hypothetically exist in the World State. Working in small groups, they created the London Hospital for the Dying, the Alpha Center for the Research and Development of the Turbine Engine, a country club called Club Aqua, and dozens of others. Once these buildings were constructed, students visited and interacted in them. Here are two examples of rooms created by Michelle, George, Matt, and Chris:

> Chapel to Our Ford
> You are in a fairly small, dimly lit, hexagon-shaped room. There is a circular table in the center with twelve chairs around it. At the head of the table is a small podium, with glowing buttons on it, and a metal T on the front. It is a console for playing synthetic music. In one corner of the room is a small, metallic refrigerator filled with bowls of soma-laced strawberry ice cream. In the center of the table is a large book of Fordism hymns. There is an exit to the lobby to the north.

> Social Gathering Room
> You are in a room where *Brave New World* citizens socialize. There is a soft glow of red light and a faint perfume of soma gas wafts

around you. The purple carpet is plush and deep purple, your feet are soothed as you walk about. There are pneumatic couches scattered about and a dance floor serviced by a synthetic music plant. Around the north and east sides a balcony runs around the room. At the south end is a well-stocked bar. You may exit north to the balcony and west to the lobby.

Those familiar with *Brave New World* will recognize that these student-created rooms illustrate some of the novel's key ideas: class distinction, consumerism, biological and psychological conditioning, and state-sponsored religion. In the Social Gathering Room, for example, students took the idea of promiscuous socialization—a major virtue in the World State—and developed a setting where such socialization would be encouraged. The plush carpeting, soft glowing lights, comfortable couches, and whiff of soma all hint that the room hosts the casual sexual encounters that Huxley satirizes.

These rooms were drawn from the text and from the imaginations of the students. In the Social Gathering Room, students programmed the hypnopaedic phrases to reflect its recreational purpose. A player who lingers here is told that "You feel a pleasantly narcotic holiday due to the soma gas" and that "The red light beckons you to the dance floor." He also hears lines from a popular song emanating from the synthetic music plant: "Hug me till you drug me honey," "Bottle of mine, it's you I've always wanted!" "Bottle of mine, why was I ever decanted?" The name of the room is also a student invention, though its bureaucratic-sounding title is pitch-perfect in its imitation of Huxley. Other student inventions were equally creative: one group developed a minor location in the novel, the London Hospital for the Dying, into a more three-dimensional space by adding a lobby and a garage for hearses. Another group reasoned that the World State relied on Alphas to develop its technology and invented a research center for the turbine engine. These elaborations illustrate that students did more than enter the novel; they reimagined and extended the story. In Wilhelm's words, they went "beyond what was stated or even suggested by the book" until "the story world [became] what could be called a 'reader's world'" (1997, 66).

Building the Conversations

Finally, my students used the *Brave New World* simulation to hold critical discussions about the novel. The simulation created an ideal environment for peer-led discussions, which took place in both informal and formal ways.

Informal discussions of the novel occasionally occurred after school or in the evening, as students logged on from home. For more structured in-class discussions, I divided students into small groups, assigned them specific topics, and, after some experimentation, created lockable rooms for each group—effectively preventing traffic in and out. The following conversation, excerpted from a small-group discussion on the role of science in the novel, illustrates how students worked together to develop a deeper understanding of this issue and the novel as a whole. You'll notice that students are writing from the point of view of the characters they created.

> Bambino says, "So is science a public danger?"
>
> Tito Hoover says, "Can be."
>
> Leroux says, "Yeah, we take science, and apply it to technology . . . technology is the result of what science teaches us."
>
> Wilhelmina Bowerman [to Bambino] "But not if it's used correctly."
>
> Bambino [to Wilhelmina Bowerman] "But it's not always used correctly, which makes it dangerous."
>
> Wilhelmina Bowerman [to Bambino] "Right on."
>
> Tito Hoover [to Bambino] "You can torture someone to see what happens and call it science."
>
> Leroux says, "Ever hear of *Frankenstein*?"
>
> Bambino says, "Like the atomic bomb."
>
> Wilhelmina Bowerman says, "Every good thing has potential for bad."
>
> Bambino says, "Not EVERY good thing, I can't think of an example off the top of my head . . . but I'm sure there is an example."
>
> Leroux says, "Like FRANKENSTEIN! He took the science he discovered (creating life), without thinking of the consequences . . . and it turned against him."
>
> Tito Hoover says, "I think that science is just the explanation of stuff and things, and how they work. Technology is taking that info and applying it to some real world principle."
>
> Wilhelmina Bowerman says, "Let's talk about that quote."
>
> Tito Hoover says, "I don't get the whole part about the truth and menace thing though?"
>
> Leroux says, "Would somebody PLEASE give me a response to that? I'm beggin' ya!"
>
> Bambino [to Leroux] "You are amazing. Right on the money. *Frankenstein* is a perfect example."

Leroux says, "Thank you!"

Wilhelmina Bowerman says, "The truth about how life was supposed to be threatened in the world state."

Tito Hoover says, "What about life and truth?"

Wilhelmina Bowerman says, "Tell me about truth."

Leroux says, "I can see that truth is a menace, at least to the World State, because if they knew the truth (that they're conditioned, have no freedom, etc.) that would probably cause them to think independently, and a large amount of W.S. citizens thinking independently of the system would definitely be a menace."

Wilhelmina Bowerman says, "Exactamundo!"

Tito Hoover says, "I no . . . understand . . . :-("

Wilhelmina Bowerman says, "And science is a public danger in the world state because science has the potential to harm people."

Leroux says, "Basically, if the W.S. citizens knew the truth about them, they'd want to make change (revolt) and that's dangerous."

Bambino says, "But science DOES exist in the W.S."

Bambino says, "I mean how do you think they created the system in the first place?"

Wilhelmina Bowerman says, "Yes, but not like how we study chemistry, bio, and physics."

Wilhelmina Bowerman says, "Even the upper castes don't know that stuff."

Bambino says, "Well the world leaders know science, just no one else."

Wilhelmina Bowerman says, "They use the chemicals in their jobs but don't know what they are."

Bambino says, "Well some aspects of science."

Wilhelmina Bowerman [to Bambino] "Right, just the high up guys."

Leroux says, "If the wrong people had access to science, they could make a soma-antidote, or create individual, free-thinking people . . . "

Leroux says, "They could disrupt the system"

Bambino says, "OMG! It might be like the US! All hell would break loose!"

Wilhelmina Bowerman says, "Right, they don't want them to have the knowledge. They only know general things."

Leroux says, "If the knowledge wasn't so restricted, there would be no W.S."

Wilhelmina Bowerman says, "The people are kept ignorant"

Tito Hoover says, "This whole thing makes me think of the *Matrix* though . . . "

Tito Hoover says, "Because towards the end they talk about how hard it will be to change other people because they are so part of the world that they couldn't believe, and . . . "

Wilhelmina Bowerman [to Tito Hoover] "What are you talking about?"

Leroux [to Tito Hoover] "I don't get your *Matrix* connections . . . "

Silent through large parts of this conversation, Tito Hoover goes on to explain his connection between the movie *The Matrix* and *Brave New World*. By listening to his classmates converse, he moved from confusion over the role of science ("I don't get the whole part about the truth and menace," he says) to his own formulation of meaning, making a subtle link between ignorance and political powerlessness. It is clear that Tito is thinking about the text in a sophisticated, analytical, and reflective way. As the conversation moves forward, his classmates realize that he sees a link that they had not seen, and they praise him for his insight.

Bambino has a similar revelation during the discussion. Midway through, he claims that "science DOES exist in the W.S." and asks, "I mean how do you think they created the system in the first place?" Here, Bambino is trying to reconcile the fact that the World State discourages science while seeming to rely on it. Both Leroux and Wilhelmina understand this paradox and explain it to Bambino. Like Tito, Bambino has begun to formulate his own interpretation, working through a textual puzzle and arriving, with the help of others, at a solution.

By allowing all to participate on equal footing, the *Brave New World* simulation encouraged students to recognize themselves as important contributors to meaning. Traditionally the final meaning of a literary text is determined hierarchically, with the author at the top, followed by literary scholars, the teacher, and the student—who is further ranked according to skill. For my students, the simulation leveled the playing field, making the production of meaning a more horizontal process. Leroux, for example, found it "helpful to be able to get a better understanding of the ideas of the chapter by learning other people's opinions." Wilhelmina added that "it was nice not to be the only one willing to share ideas."

Though many of our classrooms are already places where students feel safe to express their opinions, simulations like *Brave New World* can help the classroom become even more democratic. My own role shifted from teacher-as-source-of-knowledge to teacher-as-facilitator, lessening the resistance fostered by traditional learning hierarchies. The majority of my students felt the simulation gave them a greater voice than a traditional classroom setting, particularly in the process of meaning-making. Sometimes it is hard for teachers to give up that position as all-knowing classroom director. Bringing students into virtual worlds forces us to step back and let students direct their own learning.

■ The enCore Platform as Foundation

Of course, clicking through text-based rooms and chatting about books cannot compete with the visceral rush of stealing cars (*Grand Theft Auto*), destroying enemy combatants with a deadly personal arsenal (*Unreal Tournament*), conquering the world (*Age of Empires*), or any of the addictive virtual diversions offered by today's video games. But students are quick to pick up the chat format of the enCore platform, which is similar to instant messaging—one of the most popular means of electronic communication among teenagers. And a recent article in *Wired* argues that text-based adventures, sometimes called interactive fictions, still appeal to a following who would rather imagine than see the worlds they traverse (Ogles 2005).

Most important for literature teachers, though, is the way the enCore platform can help students become better readers by encouraging them to enter and see the story world; connect with its characters; scrutinize and expand the text; gain practice in meaning-making; and, as we will see in a moment, contextualize the text with biographical, historical, and cultural information. These are the foundational beliefs of the literature scholars developing Literary Worlds, the enCore environment created at Western Michigan University. Funded by a University Innovation Grant and based on my dissertation, the Literary Worlds project involves English department faculty, graduate students, and undergraduate students working to build a series of nonprofit literary simulations about canonical and contemporary works. Many of these free simulations are currently under development, and many are being used by high school and university literature teachers around the country.

In Allen's *Village of Umuofia*, a simulation based on Chinua Achebe's novel *Things Fall Apart*, students begin by exploring a virtual replication of an Igbo village, complete with authentic West African village music and historical photographs taken by an anthropologist who worked in the region and time the novel is set. Students then role-play as characters from the novel, attempting to experience, examine, and understand the cultural gap between the Igbo people and the British missionaries who come to evangelize and rule them. The simulation is designed for a single class period, but may be extended to several class periods (or even longer) depending on the goals of the teacher and the interest of students. Calling for students to engage in a careful reading and discussion of the novel, the *Village of Umuofia* simulation has been used in dozens of college and high school world literature classrooms—an alternative high school class in inner-city New York, a private school in Texas, an AP class in Tucson, a performing arts class in Los Angeles, and English literature classes in Tanzania and Ghana.

In another Literary Worlds simulation, doctoral student Joseph Haughey has constructed a comprehensive and playful world based on Shakespeare's *A Midsummer Night's Dream*. In his creation, whimsically titled *Midsummer Madness*, students redramatize the events of the play by role-playing as its characters. Each player is given specific tasks: the student playing the fairy Puck, for instance, must use his magic to accomplish three mischievous acts; Oberon, the king of the fairies, must unite Helena and Demetrius in marriage before the role-play finishes. By interacting with other players in the virtual Athenian wood, students actually create their own version of the play, taking advantage of the uniquely theatrical environment while gaining deeper insights into the drama. Working with undergraduates, Haughey hopes that "immersion in the virtual world inevitably leads to participants' more profound engagement with the actual play."

Other simulations promise to situate texts within rich historical and cultural contexts. In *Mrs. Dalloway's London*, designed by professor Todd Kutcha, undergraduates explore the relationship of setting and character in the novel by using maps, images, and other materials from the period to retrace the routes that two characters walk through London in the 1920s. An equally interesting simulation focusing on the fairy tale *The Pied Piper* was developed by graduate student Linda Dick. Participants try to solve the mystery concerning the source of the tale by examining a historical text thought to be its origin, reading multiple versions of the tale, and redramatizing its central events through role-play.

Developers of these and other simulations at Literary Worlds will continue to seek innovative ways of using the enCore environment, just one type of virtual reality, to teach a wide range of literary texts. Reflecting on the four key goals of literature instruction we identified in the introduction—entering

FIGURE 4–2 *Using enCore simulations in the literature classroom*

Entering	Close Reading	Contextualizing	Responding
Create and describe characters from text	Examine textual excerpts; explore how language operates	Examine historical images and documents related to the text	Role-play as characters from text
Role-play as characters from text; accomplish specific tasks as those characters	Compare text to other versions or sources	Experience multimedia enrichment such as video and music related to the text	Construct or reinvent settings of the text
Explore replications of the setting	Discuss literary elements of the text	Compare text to other versions or sources	Discuss themes or other ideas drawn from text
Construct or reinvent settings of the text	Solve textual puzzles		Discuss simulation experience compared to reading experience
	Compare textual descriptions with related visual images		

the story world, close reading, contextualizing the text, and responding to the text—we might observe that the enCore simulations described above can be used in a number of interesting ways (see Figure 4–2).

▪ Looking Ahead: Meet Me in the Metaverse

I have spent the majority of this chapter describing the enCore environment, one application Allen and I have embraced, despite occasional difficulties with access and usability (see the end of this chapter for ways of using virtual realities with limited or no technology). However, we keep one eye on the future, still waiting for a graphics-based environment as adaptable, available, and educationally valuable as the enCore tool. We look forward to the time when literary worlds of our own design can be as immersive and compelling as *World of Warcraft*, the fantasy role-playing game with millions of users worldwide. At the same time, we wonder what will be lost along the way. After all, we love good books and face-to-face conversations about them.

Such worlds have already been depicted in science fiction, perhaps most famously by Neil Stephenson in *Snow Crash*. Here the protagonist of the novel, a renowned hacker named Hiro, enters the virtual reality:

> So Hiro jacks his computer into the cigarette lighter and goggles into the Metaverse . . . . He materializes in his office, in his nice little house in the old hacker neighborhood just off the Street. It is all quite Nipponese: tatami mats cover the floor. Silvery cloud-light filters through rice-paper walls. A panel in front of him slides open to reveal a garden, complete with babbling brook and steelhead trout jumping out from time to time to grab flies. (1992, 99)

For some, what Stephenson calls the *metaverse* has already come to pass in the virtual world *Second Life*. Created by Linden Labs in 2003, *Second Life* is a massively multiplayer, three-dimensional world with (as of early 2008) over twelve million residents from all over the world. At any given time, thousands of these residents are logged in. What are they doing? Customizing their avatars (three-dimensional representations of themselves), spending *Second Life* currency in casinos or strip malls, conferencing with business colleagues, socializing with friends or special interest groups, developing their own real estate, patronizing real-world businesses like Reuters or Pontiac that have set up shop in *Second Life*, or playing in-world games designed by other residents. A basic *Second Life* account is free, and there is even a *Teen Second Life* grid for players between the ages of thirteen and seventeen.

What makes *Second Life* unique is that unlike other online games that immerse players in already-developed worlds, *Second Life* is almost entirely created by its residents. This last fact has given rise to a vigorous in-world economy. Players design and retain ownership of in-world objects, allowing them to buy, sell, and even get rich. For the industrious few, wealth inside of *Second Life* has even translated to real-world gains as real-world businesses are taking an interest in *Second Life*. It is now possible, for example, to test drive a virtual Pontiac at a *Second Life* dealership, an innovation the company hopes will attract new customers. But besides fueling entrepreneurship, the ability to create and inhabit the virtual world has important educational implications. Educators have already developed rich learning environments within this virtual world.

One compelling example of these in-world educational environments is the New Media Consortium (NMC) Campus. While much of the *Second Life* world still feels like Las Vegas—casinos, tourist traps, and sex shops still dominate the virtual landscape—the NMC Campus is a haven for teaching and learn-

FIGURE 4–3 *The NMC Campus in* Second Life

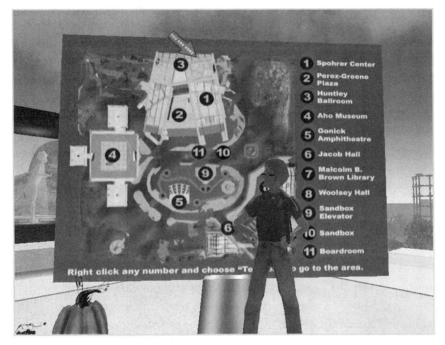

Screenshot courtesy of The New Media Consortium

ing. As seen in Figure 4–3, the campus features a large amphitheater where streaming video can be shown on giant screens, plazas, conference rooms, lecture halls, art galleries, and other accommodations. Both practical and whimsical in design, the campus hosts academic conferences, provides classroom space for NMC members, and gives virtual researchers an ideal environment to conduct fieldwork. Recently, the NMC campus has expanded and now adjoins research and teaching facilities developed by Princeton, Cornell, MIT, Colorado Tech, and other universities.

On one of my recent visits to the NMC Campus, I perused a poster display in Huntley Hall, one of the dozens of public spaces on the campus. I also watched streaming video of Al Gore speaking at the Technology, Entertainment, and Design (TED) conference, shown on the large screen in an outdoor amphitheater. There are over 5,000 members of the NMC—most hailing from universities, though nonprofit organizations and corporations are represented as well. Members meet regularly on campus to discuss teaching and learning in *Second Life*, to share their expertise, to tour new educational simulations, and to plan for upcoming conferences and events.

The NMC campus is just one part of a much larger educational community in *Second Life*. Linden Labs encourages educators to use *Second Life* for serious academic purposes. It created a *Second Life* campus where university faculty can receive one acre of free land to teach virtual courses. Offered in the upcoming semester are courses in cyberculture, virtual reality design, new media studies, game design, theater and culture, and more—all taught by professors from a range of institutions. Over fifty universities have developed similar virtual campuses, including the University of Southern California, the University of Pennsylvania, Harvard, and San Diego State University (which features a three-dimensional webquest on the American immigrant experience).

The *Teen Second Life* grid offers opportunities for secondary students (aged thirteen to seventeen) and educators. On Global Kids Island, for example, teenagers can participate in programming workshops, attend virtual summer camps, compete in digital media essay contests, and learn about global issues such as the Darfur genocide. To be sure, the technical requirements of *Second Life* make it unrealistic for most public middle and high schools; for example, to run properly the program requires a high-end graphics card, frequent updates, and a lot of bandwidth. Yet even with these challenges, *Second Life* still points to the educational promise of virtual realities.

One extraordinary simulation developed by the University of California–Davis, for example, replicates the effects of schizophrenia. Based on two case studies of individuals suffering from the disorder, the simulation subjects participants to a barrage of voices and visual distortions meant to reproduce the experience of living with the disease. Another example is the International Spaceflight Museum, where guests can view scale models of spacecraft and rockets; watch a live feed of NASA television; interact with several exhibits; and browse through resources covering astronomy, space exploration, and astrophysics. A third example, the simulation at the Svarga Artificial Life Experiment, has developed a virtual ecosystem that grows on its own and has its own climate. These and other educational sites within *Second Life* may be best *experienced* rather than described: there is no substitute for wandering through these sometimes stunning microworlds, seeing and hearing all they have to offer.

Allen and I believe that literary texts might be *experienced* in the same way. In the same way the enCore environment encourages students to see the story world and connect to its characters, *Second Life* and similar platforms might replicate literary worlds in a more graphic and—for the generation raised on video games—compelling way. What if students could reenact *Much Ado About Nothing* in a virtual Globe Theater, true in detail down to the trapdoor and cellarage? What if they could design their own setting for a modern retelling of the same play, creating appropriate costumes and stage props for their avatars? In one sense, *Second Life* is already a vast literary work, a drama with thousands of characters and story arcs. What if we took the next step and designed specific literary worlds where novels, plays, and poetry could be experienced as well as read? What if the setting of *1984* could be rendered with all of the starkness that Orwell conveys?

> Down in the street little eddies of wind were whirling dust and torn paper into spirals, and though the sun was shining and the sky a harsh blue, there seemed to be no color in anything, except the posters that were plastered everywhere. The black-moustachio'd face gazed down from every commanding corner. There was one on the house-front immediately opposite. BIG BROTHER IS WATCHING YOU, the caption said, while the dark eyes looked deep into Winston's own. (1950, 6)

Until we feel that Big Brother *is* watching us—a strange thing to wish for—Allen and I will continue to look for new ways to bring literary texts to life in digital environments. A decade ago, Janet Murray realized the potential that digital technology had to shape the way we experience and tell stories. In *Hamlet on the Holodeck*, she wrote that "the age-old desire to live out a fantasy aroused by a fictional world has been intensified by a participatory, immersive medium that promises to satisfy it more completely than has ever before been possible" (1998, 98). Entangled as we are in these fictional worlds, we owe it to ourselves and our students to explore new ways of entering them.

Using Virtual Realities with Limited or No Technology Resources

Of all the technologies we describe in this book, virtual realities may seem the least likely choice for a teacher with limited or no technology. A three-dimensional multi-user environment such as *Second Life*, after all, might seem off-limits to a school without a lab full of new computers equipped with the latest video cards. But with a little imagination, the experiences of virtual reality can be imitated in a classroom with only one or even no computers.

- In a one-computer classroom, you can show a virtual world on the data projector, an experience that can be quite rich for students if you examine museum-like realities such as Todd Kutcha's recreation of 1920s London at Literary Worlds or the J. R. R. Tolkien Education Center in *Second Life*. Using a single laptop and a portable data projector, we have given demos on virtual realities at state and national conferences and are always taken by the power they have to captivate our audiences. Without any computers, students can still engage in role-playing activities that might be brief (character interviews, freeze frames) or sustained (live action role-plays), depending on the context.

- As video games continue to gain popularity, the idea of gaming itself becomes a useful metaphor for literature instruction, even when computers are not present. Students might write or talk about how a literary work might play as a video game; how playing a video game compares to reading a book; or how video games and literary texts share certain generic features, such as narrative, perspective, plot, characters, setting, and more. If *Lord of the Flies* were a video game, for example, would it be a first-person shooter—with every man (or boy) for himself and only sticks, fire, and the occasional rolling rock for weapons? Or would it be a strategy game, in which players would have to manage the resources of the island, deciding which units would hunt and which would tend the fire? We may find these questions slightly sacrilegious, but we are willing to entertain them because we know that gaming is a big part of our students' lives, thoughts, and language, even when they are away from their machines.

Web Resources Mentioned in Chapter 4

Literary Worlds EnCore Environment

Literary Worlds (www.literaryworlds.org) is an enCore environment hosted by Western Michigan University. Designed by faculty and graduate students in the English and English education programs, it features over a dozen literary simulations based on a range of canonical and contemporary works, including the following:

- *Angel's Space* allows students to examine the cultural contexts of Tony Kushner's play, *Angels in America*. Designed by Steve Feffer.

- *Bigger's World* takes students into the racially charged inner city of Chicago's South Side based on Richard Wright's 1940 novel, *Native Son*. Designed by Casey McKittrick.

- *Brave New World* replicates the setting of Aldous Huxley's novel and allows students to design and role-play as characters. Designed by Robert Rozema.

- *Dickens' London* is a portal to nineteenth-century London as seen through the eyes of Charles Dickens' characters. Designed by Todd Bannon.

- *Gatsby's American Dream* allows students in groups of four acting as "shades" of the novel's characters to reexamine places and events from the novel. Designed by Meghan Dykema.

- *Inismore* lets students explore the historical and political issues in the relationship of Ireland and England as examined in Lady Morgan Sydney Owenson's novel *The Wild Irish Girl: A National Tale*. Designed by Christopher Nagle.

- *Island Barrio* takes you into the world of a Puerto Rican community in New York and on the island, based on the collection of stories *An Island Like You* by Judith Ortiz Cofer. Designed by Gwen Tarbox.

- *Lord of the Flies*, a recreation of the island where the boys are lost. Allows for role-play and writing in character. Designed by Cara Arver.

- *Mice, Men and Migrant Labor* lets students compare and contrast migrant labor experience in John Steinbeck's famous novel set in 1930s California with Mexican-American migrant labor today. Designed by Gretchen Voskuil.

- *Middangeard* is an environment where students can explore the worldviews and experiences suggested by Anglo-Saxon poetry and investigate objects (artifacts, manuscripts) of Anglo-Saxon material culture. Designed by Ilse Schwietzer.

- *Midsummer Madness* is a role-playing game in which students take on the role of characters in one of Shakespeare's most delightful works, *A Midsummer Night's Dream*. Designed by Joe Haughey.

- *Moll's World* examines eighteenth-century British culture as it intersects Daniel Defoe's *Moll Flanders*. Designed by Cynthia Klekar.

- *The Tempest* lets students interact as characters lost on a desert island haunted by magical forces. Designed by Tim Heacock, Jennifer Barnes, and Allen Webb.

- *Thoughtcrime* is a game of political intrigue based in the frightening world of Orwell's *1984*. Designed by Robert Rozema.

- *Village of Umuofia,* based on Chinua Achebe's *Things Fall Apart,* incorporates an archive of black-and-white images of Ibo villages and traditional music with a role-play where students become characters interacting as traditional Africans and arriving British colonizers. Designed by Allen Webb.

Second Life Multi-User Virtual Environment

Second Life (www.secondlife.com) is a three-dimensional virtual environment with millions of registered users. *Second Life* requires a high-speed Internet connection and a high-end graphics card. Basic accounts are free. Interesting educational hotspots within *Second Life* include:

- Eduisland

- Glidden Campus

- Global Kids Island

- ICT Library

- InfoIsland

- International Spaceflight Museum

- New Globe Theater

- New Media Consortium Campus

- San Diego State University Campus

- Second Life Campus

- Second Life Library 2.0

- Svarga Artificial Life Simulation

- Virtual Hallucinations

To learn more about education in *Second Life,* please see the following:

- New Media Consortium Campus Observer (http://sl.nmc.org)

- Second Life Education (www.secondlife.com/education)

- Second Life Education Wiki (www.secondlife.com/educationwiki)

- SimTeach (www.simteach.com)

- Teen Grid (www.teen.secondlife.com)

Online Orchestration: Establishing an Effective Web Presence

5

Robert Rozema and Allen Webb

*Wiring schools alone is not enough to compensate for other factors that are fail-
ing to ensure that all students have free and equal access to both information
technology and digitized information. That will come out of endeavors that seek
to ensure . . . that the model of education as a whole is changed. This requires
retraining of teachers.*

—Donald Tapscott, *Growing Up Digital* (1998)

I t is with no small degree of skepticism that Harper Lee, through the voice
of her narrator Scout, regards her public school education in a small
southern town. In her much-loved novel *To Kill a Mockingbird*, Lee writes
that her days in school "were an endless Project that slowly evolved into a
Unit, in which miles of construction paper and wax crayon were expended
by the State of Alabama in its well-meaning but fruitless efforts to teach me
Group Dynamics. . . . As I inched sluggishly along the treadmill of the May-
comb County school system, I could not help receiving the impression that I
was being cheated out of something" (1988, 32–33). Though gentle in intent,
Lee's satire offers two warnings for educators integrating technology into their
teaching. First, it shows us just how slowly educational practices change. With
their bureaucratically capitalized letters, "Project" and "Unit" sound strik-
ingly contemporary, despite the decades gone by since Lee was a schoolgirl in
Alabama. As has facetiously been observed, if Rip Van Winkle were to wake
up today after sleeping for 130 years, the only thing he might recognize is
the public school classroom, at least in the traditional way that teaching and
learning still occur. Slow change, then, is one obstacle we might encounter
when introducing new technologies into our teaching.

And yet we know that as more and more technology streams into our schools, things *are* changing, and this fact leads to Lee's second and more important warning. No matter how much faith we put in new educational technologies, new tools can never replace or guarantee effective teaching. If miles of construction paper and wax crayons could not make Scout take interest in school, then we should not expect laptops and data projectors to do any better—unless these tools are used by expert teachers in creative ways that are rooted in effective literature and writing instruction. Amid the hype that has accompanied the deluge of technology into schools, this key idea—that technology depends on the teachers using it—is sometimes forgotten. Public school teachers and university instructors need more time, better support, and more relevant professional development in order to integrate technology into their courses (Oppenheimer 2003). This is especially true of teachers in schools with low-income and minority populations. Kathleen Fulton and Robert Sibley consider this lack of teacher expertise one of the most significant barriers to digital equity:

> The issue is deeper than one of training, and goes to the heart of teachers' belief about best ways to teach. . . . Teachers teach as they were taught; if technology was not in the picture when they were in school, it is difficult for some teachers to appreciate its value as a critical element for enhancing student learning. . . . These pedagogical barriers are creating a "didactic divide" that represents inequalities in instructional practice. (2003, 19)

What Scout was missing, then, might have been a teacher who could use the tools at her disposal to make learning more meaningful. We believe that English teachers and students can benefit from Internet technology, and we hope this book has helped you to imagine the possibilities of using Web tools in your own teaching. As we have tried to illustrate, such imagining must go beyond the mastery of select technology skills isolated from the context and content of teaching. It is not enough to be able to send an e-mail with an attachment, listen to a podcast, or set up a blog. Knowing *how* to do these things has value, but understanding *why* is more important. In this chapter, we offer our comprehensive ideas for a Web-enriched English language arts classroom, a classroom where the *how* and *why* of technology come together under the guidance of an expert English teacher. Our picture may seem quaint and curious two decades from now, as the applications that are new today become commonplace and then, perhaps, fade into obsolescence. Still we hope that our *ideas* about the technology-enriched classroom have lasting value. This chapter describes two platforms for tying together all of the technologies we have explored thus far: the class website and the class blog. After examining how we use these platforms to integrate text archives, threaded discussions, blogs, podcasts, feed readers, and more into our teaching, we'll talk about how they fit into the English classroom of the future—a wireless and highly flexible learning environment that has already appeared at many universities and schools.

■ The Website as Class Syllabus (Allen Webb)

Teaching in the technologically enriched English classroom involves a range of new activities and approaches, many of them described in this book. While Rob and I value established methods of literature instruction, we know that the classroom of the future invites teachers and students to explore new possibilities. But how can we take advantage of these possibilities? We believe teachers will be better able to do so by creating a *Web presence*—that is, by moving online and establishing home bases on the Web.

Case Study: African Literature

I have found class websites with online syllabi to be an effective way to create a Web presence that supports the teaching of literature. I create a class website for every class I teach; as I teach classes for a second and third time the site grows, changes, and improves. As an example, let me discuss the online syllabus for my African literature class, currently available on my website (www.allenwebb.net; see Figure 5–1). At first glance, the syllabus looks like that of any college literature course. It lists required texts, details the reading schedule, explains assignments, and provides due dates. It lists my office hours and my email address. It sets forward rules about attendance, grading, and academic honesty. But in a number of important ways, this syllabus goes well beyond the typical printed version.

I have discovered that most of my students enter my African literature class knowing very little about Africa, let alone African literature. So the syllabus is enriched with images and links that introduce students to Africa and to the themes of the course. Images taken with permission from the National Museum of African Art (a simple email request to the site owner) are linked back to the museum, including one that shows a group of African students in an African school using traditional African learning boards. Images of African musical instruments are linked to sites that feature African music; an image of a traditional African eating bowl links to information about a Nigerian

FIGURE 5–1 *Allen's class website*

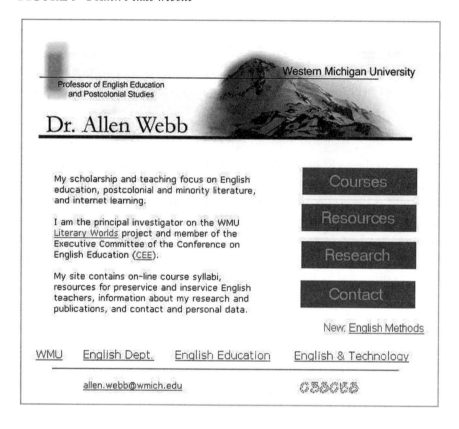

restaurant in town. The syllabus also links to a site I created about African films that are available through our university library.

To encourage my students to stay current on African news, the syllabus also links to AllAfrica.com, the largest electronic distributor of African news and information worldwide. Registered in Mauritius (with offices in Johannesburg, Dakar, Lagos, and Washington D.C.), AllAfrica is one of a family of companies that aggregates, produces, and distributes news from across Africa to tens of millions of readers. My syllabus also links to student organizations at the university, including the Muslim Student Association and the African Student Organization, and features events where my students can meet Africans living in our community and attend a variety of cultural activities and events. There are links to resources about AIDS in Africa, the impact of global warming on Africa, and the controversy over female genital mutilation. These are just some of the cultural links that students encounter every time they check the syllabus.

These resources help my students learn about the social, cultural, and political contexts of the literature they are reading. I begin class by having students study African geography and political history. Links from the syllabus take students to informative sites created by Michigan State University's African Research Center and the BBC's Story of Africa site. Before students visit these sites, I provide them with specific questions to guide their exploration—they know that I will later use these same questions to prompt in-class writing. I also take advantage of the African folklore resource in the Internet Sacred Text Archive that I describe in Chapter 1. I want students to know the names and locations of the countries of Africa, so my syllabus includes a map of Africa and links to an online quiz on this information. I ask students to select from a number of "African Exploration Activities" including viewing online video, listening to music, reading blogs, and more. The same range of exploration activities created for this African literature course can be found online for *any* literature course. After all, America of the nineteenth century (for instance) may be an almost equally exotic, unknown territory to our students!

Like many professors of African literature, I ask my students to read (and write a paper on) Chinua Achebe's famous novel *Things Fall Apart*. My online syllabus includes links to a variety of sites on the novel, including reading questions, study guides, and background on the author created by scholars of African literature. The syllabus is also linked to a virtual reality role-play on the novel that I created and that Rob describes in Chapter 4 of this book. Because *Things Fall Apart* is so widely taught, there are dozens of places where students can buy or download essays about the novel—MyTermPapers.com, DigitalTermPapers.com, MegaEssay.com, Africanlit.com, and even a site specifically titled ThingsFallApart.com that offers hundreds of papers on the novel (all for only $9.95 per page). The ease of plagiarism makes it awfully tempting! How do I cope with the availability of term papers on the Web? I deliberately post links to all of these sites on my class website, along with the following caveat:

> Yes, there are student papers on *Things Fall Apart* available online. These are papers some students try to turn in as their own work. Some of these papers do have interesting ideas and are easier to read than real scholarship. You may look at student essays, but remember that the point is for you to do your own work. If you read other people's work you MUST properly cite it and list it in your bibliography—otherwise, you are committing plagiarism. Just so you know, I am good at detecting plagiarism, finding the source, and ensuring that students who plagiarize learn their lesson.

Of course, ready-made essays are available on almost any text an English teacher is likely to assign. Alas we now need to be increasingly savvy detecting plagiarism, leading some of us to use services like TurnItIn.com. Since I don't think we can stop students from finding such papers, I believe it is better to show them how to use them—if at all—with responsibility and care. A teacher Web presence can help make this possible.

Reading literary scholarship can be helpful for advanced students as they develop their thinking about a particular text. For this college African literature class, I required that students seeking an "A" on their paper read real scholarship—not papers for sale online, but the kind traditionally available only in scholarly journals held in academic libraries. Although I believe it is important for students to venture to the library to broaden and deepen the range of scholarly work they can draw on, academic journals in literary studies have become available online in the last few years. Therefore the paper assignment page of my class site has information and links explaining how to access scholarly journals. The same page also explains how to use the Modern Language Association (MLA) database to find full-text articles. Unlike student papers for sale, these are articles in responsible, peer-reviewed journals such as *Research in African Literature, College Literature,* and *Studies in the Novel.* The availability of these articles is a great motivator.

Having an online syllabus facilitates the fluid integration of a broad range of class content and activities. The syllabus can include links to teaching resources for specific literary works on the Web—not only scholarly journals but also textual archives, information on works and authors, cultural and historical background sites, visual depictions of settings (see, for example, the Literary Locales site developed by San Jose State University), webquests, lesson plans, study guides, hypertexts, and more.

My Web presence also lets me foster student reading beyond the class texts. During the last four weeks of my African literature course, my students form literature circles of four to six students and select books they want to explore from a long list. (For more on this approach see LiteratureCircles.com.) Some students decided to read the works of a particular author or to focus on the literature of a particular country. Others chose their reading based on theme or topical interest. Others dabbled. Having the freedom to choose their reading is empowering and, unfortunately, all too rare in school. The class also used our online discussion forum to share thoughts about and reactions to the novels. Although I might have created separate prompts for the students to share with their small groups, I chose instead to create a single prompt where students posted comments for the whole class. It was wonderful to watch students share their enthusiasm for the novels they had selected with the rest of the class.

> 15:6) Author: Tara
> It's nice to meet in literature circles to gather ideas and check for understanding and comprehension with group members about what we are reading. It's kind of fun reading from one specific author and getting to know his style. I am liking *Anthills of the Savannah*, although it's a hard read. Warning: the point of view changes a lot so be prepared.

> 15:10) Author: Brian
> I enjoyed these literature circles. The fact that you got to choose your books was great because some of the books seemed really interesting to me and some of them did not. It also helped that I had a helpful and extremely smart group. We read some African children's literature, *Second Class Citizen*, and *Dark Child*. I especially enjoyed the children's literature because of the illustrations in the books. The artwork was wonderful.

> 15:11) Author: Tonya
> I like working in the literature circles. When I was unable to attend class my group was awesome about keeping in touch with me. We communicated well and were able to dive deep in to the novels. I liked that we explored them thoroughly, looking beyond the surface. For my final project, I developed teaching units about the novels. I enjoyed thinking of the questions to ask my future students and imagining how they would respond. The literature circle helped me navigate and develop my ideas.

The reading list that students could choose from for the literature circle reading was posted to the class site and each novel listed linked to Amazon.com —where they could not only purchase the book, but also read reviews before they decided which books they wanted to read. I also provided the email addresses of five different professors of African literature—three addresses of African professors in the United States and two addresses of professors living in Senegal—whom my students could email to get additional reading recommendations. The literature circle assignment page included links to recommended book lists that others had created as well as links to additional African literature syllabi from courses and professors around the world.

Adding a list of course syllabi from other universities to my class site is now something that I do for every class I teach. It is not hard to find such syllabi: just search Google to see what comes up. The page I created for syllabi of African literature courses included links to seventeen different classes at universities—from Central Oregon Community College to Oberlin, from Allegany College to the University of Wisconsin, from the University of Harare in Zimbabwe to the University of the Witwaterstrand in Johannesburg. Comparing syllabi from teachers or professors at different schools helps students better understand their own education and question the idea that literature courses have a single acceptable canon. I sometimes use lists of such syllabi as the focus of a final exam in which students compare the course they have taken to similar courses they might take elsewhere. Opportunities for this kind of meta-reflection are becoming more common as more teachers and professors publish their syllabi on the Web. And of course, the same approach is possible on the secondary level—it could include class sites and course syllabi, textbook sites from different publishers, and additional secondary textbook resources such as BeyondBooks.com.

Syllabi: The Broader Context

Creating an online syllabus or class website is becoming easier and easier. For years, I used design programs such as Dreamweaver, Frontpage, or Netscape Composer to teach current and pre-service teachers the principles of Web design (Microsoft Word can also be used). Once my students' pages were created, they were uploaded to the university Web server. Schools and universities typically have servers, but teachers may want their site to be independent; Webpages can be hosted at many different free and proprietary services.

Today, advances on the Web make publishing sites even simpler. In the summer of 2007, all of my students made websites at Google Pages, which provides easy-to-use online editors and templates as well as free hosting. With Google Pages, you don't need any software—only access to the Internet. The same is true of many wiki sites, where teachers can publish websites and syllabi, host discussion boards, and create collaborative online writing projects for their students. Any website you create will have an address depending on the server it is stored on, but you can also purchase any available Web address for about eight dollars per year (mine is www.allenwebb.net) and use that address to forward browsers to your server.

For the last ten years, the practicing and aspiring English teachers in my classes have created a Web presence by developing their own teaching websites. Making a site is a completely new idea to nearly all of my students, and yet they are able to start their sites in one class meeting and, in less than two weeks, have something they are really proud of. Their sites are creative and have a consistent look or theme that speaks to their interests. Each site includes at least a dozen pages, some directed to students, some to parents, some to colleagues, and some personal pages where they share information about their interests and family. The pages include many images and often have interesting backgrounds. The pages include recommended reading lists for their students, links to resources for parents and colleagues, drafts of online syllabi for classes that they hope to teach, statements of teaching philosophy, and portfolios of work from previous courses. You can find examples of their work at the Teaching English Through Technology site, a website Rob and I created in 2002. For not-yet-employed teachers, class websites are great to show off at job interviews—far better than the traditional portfolio since they are a living document targeted to their future students that demonstrate their ability to meaningfully integrate technology into English teaching.

Both Rob and I believe that Web publishing has become a basic writing skill for both teachers and students. Certainly everything that we have learned about the teaching of composition over the course of the last generation points to the importance of publishing. We talk a lot in English classes about going beyond just writing for the teacher. Drawing on movements such as Foxfire and the Writing Project, students have produced class publications, magazines, and chapbooks—and have even submitted their creative work to professional journals. Now all of this kind of publishing can be done on the Web, creating publications that are accessible to anyone in the world with an Internet connection. Students can learn to publish their own writing, create their own websites, and develop collaborative Web publishing projects from content-based sites to poetry e-zines to wikis. Students can keep blogs, record podcasts, and produce digital videos that can be shared with huge audiences via sites such as iTunes and YouTube. As English teachers in the twenty-first century, we can help our students become literate in a wide range of communication formats and technologies that are shaping the creative arts, the business world, and the very functions and practices of a democratic society. A class website is an important step in this direction.

■ The Class Blog as Evolving Conversation (Robert Rozema)

Like Allen, I have a home base on the Web, a place where my students can access course resources, read news and announcements pertaining to the class, find archives of student projects from previous semesters, and do much more.

While Allen creates his sites with Web design software, I rely on another flexible tool—the blog—to achieve many of the same purposes. I use the Wordpress blogging platform, one of many blogging services available for free on the Web. The title of my blog, Secondary Worlds, alludes to J. R. R. Tolkien's term for the imaginary realms of fairy tales; to the idea that technology offers us new worlds to explore; and finally, to the intended audience of the blog—future secondary English teachers. I often spend the first day of class illustrating just how my blog works. In doing so I underscore that Secondary Worlds has several functions—acting as my own academic blog, a reservoir of course resources, and a nerve center that connects all of my students' blogs together.

As an academic blog, Secondary Worlds is dedicated to topics related to teaching, technology, and English language arts. Other academic blogs are focused on similar issues: Will Richardson's Weblogg-ed and Troy Hicks' Digital Writing, Digital Teaching, to cite two examples, both approach English education from a technological perspective. And like these academic blogs, Secondary Worlds is a sort of hybrid—a blend of the genres originally described by Rebecca Blood in her pioneering text *The Weblog Handbook* (2002). I have found that discussing the different genres of blogs is an important first step toward helping my students understand my blog and getting them to write with purpose on their own blogs, which they are required to keep throughout the semester.

Writing in 2002, Blood defined three dominant blog genres: the personal journal, the notebook, and the filter blog. The personal journal—the form of blogging popularized by services like Blogger, Xanga, and Livejournal—is a diarylike blog that records daily events in the life of the writer. Typically read by a handful of friends, personal journals are considered *sticky*, since they attempt to retain readers rather than redirect them via links to other sites or blogs. In contrast, the chief purpose of the second genre—the notebook blog—is to record *ideas* rather than daily events. Notebook blog entries are typically longer and more carefully considered than journal entries, and notebooks frequently link to sites to illustrate points or support arguments. Finally, the filter blog amasses interesting links, pointing to online resources with only minimal commentary from the author. Today media-savvy bloggers have expanded the idea of the filter by using their blogs to point to online articles from major news sources, often interspersing clips from the articles with commentary or critique.

An academic blog such as Secondary Worlds may include some personal reflection like a journal blog, but it is typically focused on a topic or series of topics (like a notebook blog) and it actively points to online resources (like a filter blog). As I discuss in Chapter 3, I use a feed reader to find these resources—subscribing to feeds from major newspapers, other blogs, and podcasts. My blog then becomes a platform to evaluate, critique, and link to articles on teaching, technology, and the English language arts. Other academic blogs written by professors and teachers follow these same conventions as their writers find interesting or provocative articles, excerpt them, and provide analysis.

The screen capture of my blog (Figure 5–2) illustrates how this works. Here I am responding to a report on Internet safety conducted by C. S. Mott

FIGURE 5–2 *Rob's class blog*

Children's Hospital. After introducing the report, I give a brief analysis and excerpt a large section of the article, offsetting the quoted material in a grey block quote to distinguish it from my own writing. I also cite the article completely and link to the original source, so readers can follow through to the full article. Past entries on Secondary Worlds have covered many of the topics in this book, including virtual realities, blogging, podcasting, and text archives.

I post entries once or twice per week, using my blog to keep my students updated on issues related to teaching English and technology and, just as importantly, to model effective technology integration in an English language arts context. Research demonstrates that technology training for pre-service teachers is most successful when it occurs in all teacher education courses, when expert teacher education faculty model how to use technology, and when pre-service teachers are supervised by mentor teachers who support and encourage them as they use technology during their field experiences (Moursund and Bielefeldt 1999). I want my blog to serve as a model for secondary teachers through all of their preparatory coursework and field experiences. More specifically, Secondary Worlds provides a ready illustration of one key assignment they must complete in my methods course—their own academic blog.

To create academic blogs, my students use Edublogs, a free service that runs on the Wordpress blogging platform. In addition to offering a range of sharp templates, Edublogs provides users with a wealth of free features and helpful support. At the same time, students set up accounts at Google Reader, a powerful feed reader that collects headlines from news sources all over the Web (see Chapter 3 for more on how this application works). I believe that feed readers are an essential part of academic blogging. As David Parry argues,

> Teaching students to write blogs without at least providing the idea behind RSS is like teaching them to write papers on word processors, but never showing them how to use spell check, find and replace, italics or any of the formatting tools; it just repeats the prior technical moment of writing. Rather than simply referring to an article, students need to author documents that link to that article, and link to those articles in a way that enhances their writing. (2006)

The main purpose of the academic blog is for my students to stay current on topics that are important to our discipline. They do so by reading articles gathered by their feed reader and by posting responses to these articles on their blogs. My students focus their blogs on topics related to English language arts instruction: censorship and literature, standardized testing, writing assessment, plagiarism, or second language acquisition. I do caution students that they may need to narrow or switch topics as the semester progresses, depending on how many news items their feed readers are yielding. In the past, students have begun with a large idea (e.g., young adult literature) and found a more specific subtopic (e.g., young adult "chick" literature such as the *Gossip Girls* series) as articles began streaming in.

To encourage students to read a variety of sources, I also require them to subscribe to at least two major news outlets such as the *New York Times* or BBC News; at least one major search query through Google News (e.g., *MySpace schools*); at least one blog that deals specifically with their topic (e.g., Andy Carvin's Learning Now); and finally all of their classmates' blogs, on which they comment throughout the semester. Then I provide the guidelines shown in Figure 5–3 for their academic blogs.

Tami, a student in my Teaching Writing course, dedicated her academic blog to issues related to English language learners in secondary schools. In the post shown in Figure 5–4, Tami linked to an article in the *Columbus Dispatch* and used the information she found there to raise questions about her undergraduate teacher education at my university: Will she need ESL certification to teach English? If so, why is she required to take just one linguistics course? Her post illustrates that the academic blog assignment helps students to stay on top of

FIGURE 5–3 *Academic blog requirements*

- An opening statement in which you identify your topic, describe what you hope to learn about it, list your feeds, and explain why you chose the feed you did.

- Eight 300-to 500-word posts that draw on at least one article each. Each post should include key excerpts from the article, a complete citation of the article, and a functional link to the original article. Most of the post should be dedicated to your response to the ideas presented in the article.

- A closing statement in which you reflect on what you have learned about your topic and what you think about RSS technology.

- At least ten 200-word comments on your classmates' blogs.

- A complete blogroll of your classmates' blogs, a link to Google Reader, categories if you cover multiple topics, a visible RSS icon for easy syndication, and readable font and pleasing aesthetics.

FIGURE 5–4 *Tami's academic blog*

Home | About |

The only thing to do is jump over the moon...
The musings of a future teacher.

Implications for the lowly undergraduate students.

February 25, 2007

Posted by tamiteshima under News

I used to think it was funny when my Teaching ESL (ENG 365) professor would say to all of us, "You know, after taking this class, most of you are going to be more knowledgable about teaching ESL students than teachers teaching ESL students are right now." I laughed then, but after reading an article from the Columbus Dispatch, I'm starting to think maybe she was right.

The need ESL education has been skyrocketing over the past decade. In in the 2005-2006 school year, Ohio employed only 218 teachers with an ESL endorsement. Between these 218 teachers, there were 25,000 ESL students. If I'm doing the math correctly, that's about 115 students per teacher. That doesn't seem like much, especially since classroom size is about 20-30 kids, with approximately five preps in one day. However, this number assumes that each teacher is teaching the exact same number of students, when it is most likely that some are teaching less while others are teaching many more. It also assumes that there is an ESL teacher where ESL students are. This might not be true.

Now that I've finished that tangent (sorry), let me return to the article. Basically, Ohio is in need of ESL teachers, as is the rest of the United States.

> Westerville's ESL population has swelled from 73 to 1,244 students in a decade. Whitehall was nearly void of ESL students in the mid-1990s. Now, they make up more than 11 percent of the student body, according to Ohio Department of Education data.
>
> The state requires teachers to have an endorsement or license in ESL if they are teaching a class to help students learn English. If they are teaching a specific subject, such as math or history, to a class of ESL students, a state endorsement is preferred but not required, department spokesman J.C. Benton said.
>
> Finding enough qualified teachers to handle the demand has been challenging, school officials say.
>
> "They are few and far between," said Beverly Good, Westerville schools' ESL coordinator. "There are more students spread between fewer teachers because they're so hard to find."

So, if there's such a demand for ESL teachers, why aren't we receiving better preparation for teaching ESL students while we're in undergrad? The only class offered in undergraduate studies at GVSU for English and modern language majors (not *education* majors, mind you) to help in teaching ESL is ENG 365, and the Category F classes all deal with grammar and linguistics. Students receiving a degree in education five years ago weren't required to do *that* even, and now they're losing their jobs. ESL students weren't as abundant then or before then, but they are now. So if we're all going to encounter ESL students in our classrooms, why not give us something to go on, huh?

My point is this — if schools are demanding teachers that need to be able to teach something other than general education classes, colleges need to prepare undergrads to do so. Otherwise, we're all either boggled as to how to teach these students or left without a job, and both are pretty darn scary.

Demand for ESL teachers growing
by Simone Sebastian
Columbus Dispatch
Full article

Archived Entry

Post Date :
February 25, 2007 at 9:47 pm
Category :
News
Do More :
You can leave a response, or trackback from your own site.

current issues in the field. Other students raised equally relevant questions on their academic blogs: How does critical pedagogy work in a suburban setting? Does standardized testing devalue the writing process? Is ability-level tracking discriminatory against minority and low-income students? To explore these questions, students read and respond to a wide range of articles drawn from sources they might not have read without the assignment.

I also like to use student blog entries to enrich my teaching, relating current events to the topics of my classes. For example, the same week Tami was weighing the possibility of needing an ESL endorsement to teach English, my department was considering requiring an upper-level linguistics course for all its English education majors. I took advantage of this coincidence to pursue the issue in my writing methods class. In the same course, I used a student post about TurnItIn.com, the antiplagiarism software used by my university and a frequent topic for student blog entries, to start a conversation about creating a writing community—and to talk about how such software can destroy the mutual trust necessary for such a community to exist.

The academic blog assignment also gives students a means to establish their own presence on the Web, which as we have argued, is becoming essential to teaching English. Future teachers like Tami enter the profession with a well-defined and intellectually serious online presence. Current teachers are already using academic blogs as home bases on the Web. For example, Lisa Rozema, an English teacher in Michigan, has used academic blogs for the past two semesters to help her juniors and seniors find topics for their research essays. Her students start by subscribing to a range of news sources, then work through the semester to find a possible focus while keeping an annotated record of their ideas on their blogs. A student might begin with a broad interest in science; write brief responses to articles on nanotechnology, space exploration, and other related issues; and eventually decide on climate crisis as a subject for research. Lisa keeps her own blog, using it to point to successful student entries in the same way that I do on Secondary Worlds.

The Blog as Resource

Beyond serving as a model for academic blogging, my blog provides course resources and a space for publishing student work. Many blogging services now allow users to create pages apart from the main blog entries, making it easier than ever to keep a class blog. Using Wordpress, for example, I create separate course pages to store this more permanent information. These course pages link to documents, such as the course syllabus or PowerPoint presentations, which students can download if they lose the original document or miss a lecture. Other links point to online articles such as "A Study of High School Literature Anthologies," an in-depth research report by Arthur Applebee that we use to evaluate commercial literature anthologies. In the same way that Allen's online syllabi include links to outstanding Web resources, I provide links to a range of Web materials—software downloads necessary for course assignments, student blogs from previous semesters, other Web projects I have developed, information on state and national conference opportunities, and even previous entries that students found helpful in the past. And of course I link to all of my student blogs, positioning Secondary Worlds at the center of a large, interconnected class text that grows as the semester progresses. My students have even taken to calling my blog the *mother blog*.

My blog also offers screencast tutorials for students who need technical assistance on class projects. A *screencast* is simply a short movie of a computer screen, typically created to illustrate how a particular application works. The movie of the screen is accompanied by a voiceover narrative that explains what is happening. Because my classes use both Google Reader and Wordpress, I have developed screencasts (each six or seven minutes long that show the program in action) for both of these applications. Screencasts are surprisingly easy to make; I use a free program called Windows Media Encoder to capture the screen and an inexpensive microphone to record the narration. Essentially, making a screencast involves starting Windows Media Encoder and talking through what you are doing on screen—using Google Reader, setting up a Wordpress blog, or editing an Audacity track. Once completed, a screencast may be uploaded to a blog, YouTube, or a social network. I publish my screencasts to Secondary Worlds. Students can download and view them on software such as Windows Media Player or Real Player. Screencasts ideally give students the technical answers they are looking for and save them a trip to the computer help center.

Finally, unlike the traditional site in which information moves unidirectionally from teacher to student, Secondary Worlds features student-created content. Each semester my students produce podcasts based on young adult novels, a process described in detail in Chapter 3. When the podcasts are finished, I upload them to Secondary Worlds, where they may be listened to or downloaded. In addition to providing an archive of examples for future students, the published podcasts also serve to interest these students in various young adult novels—including *The Chocolate War, Monster, Feed, Speak, Jake Reinvented,* and more. Since my students read at least three young adult novels for their literature circle groups, the podcasts published on my site find a lasting audience of students in subsequent courses.

As a teaching tool, then, Secondary Worlds offers students a model of academic blogging and provides course resources and content. Teaching in a fairly traditional classroom with a single instructor station and accompanying overhead data projector, I frequently display Secondary Worlds on the big screen, using the blog to point to exemplary student writing, start class discussions, critique articles, examine helpful online resources, embed videos from YouTube, listen to podcasts, view screencasts, and demonstrate tools like Google Reader or Wordpress. Indeed both the class blog and the class website described above are well-suited for a classroom with fairly limited technology—perhaps only a single computer and a data projector, as in my case, or even a teacher laptop with a portable data projector borrowed from the media center. These tools become even more engaging, however, in the wireless classrooms now emerging in schools and universities.

▦ Looking Ahead: The Wireless English Classroom

In the winter of 2002, the English education program at Western Michigan University began teaching classes in the newly constructed English Education Laboratory (EEL), a wireless classroom nearly two years in the making. The EEL is furnished with twenty-four student laptops stored in two portable carts, three desktop computers equipped with scanners, an overhead data projector, digital cameras, a smart board, and printers. The laptops are networked to the data projector, so students can display content from their laptop to the rest of the class with ease. The lab also features tables and chairs on casters that can be easily rearranged into rows, small circles, theater seating, or other large group formations. Allen, the designer of this room, envisioned a flexible and comfortable environment where future and present English teachers could experience the integration of technology into literature and composition teaching. We think that this kind of wireless, laptop environment will be typical of the English classroom of the future. Working in this environment, English education undergraduates at Western Michigan University gain experience with technologies that are increasingly available in public schools.

The creation of the EEL, among the first of its kind in a major public university, was one small ripple in what has been called the wireless revolution, the large-scale movement toward wireless computing that began on college campuses in about the year 2000. Today about half of all college classrooms are covered by wireless networks (Bugeja 2007), and almost every college campus has at least limited wireless connectivity. For many universities and public schools, choosing a wireless network is a smart economic decision, since setting up the access points that constitute a wireless network is much cheaper than retrofitting old buildings with high-speed cables. On average, schools spend about one-fifth the amount on wireless as they would have on wired connections (Carlson 2000).

Beyond these financial considerations, universities are discovering that mobile computing is an essential part of college life, both for students and faculty. For students, owning a wireless-enabled laptop is becoming more and more necessary to the degree that many universities offer student discounts on laptops and wireless cards. Faculty members are given similar incentives to purchase laptops in order to take advantage of campuswide wireless networks. Covering all locations on campus—from the student union to the laboratories to the dorms—such wireless networks allow users to communicate with one another, share resources and ideas, download podcasts of lectures, publish content to the Web, access university databases, register for classes, take part in online courses, and much more. While the presence of laptops in lecture halls has occasionally exasperated professors who see students checking their email, updating their Facebook profiles, or surfing the Web during class, it seems clear that mobile computing has significant implications for teaching and learning.

Wireless networks are also becoming more common on secondary and elementary campuses, with 45 percent of public schools in 2005 offering at least partial wireless coverage (Wells and Lewis 2006). Of course, wireless networks work only when students have access to wireless-enabled laptops, and in this area K–12 schools are still lagging behind. Most schools possess at least one laptop cart—sometimes called a C.O.W. for *computer on wheels*—which serves as a mobile wireless access point and typically houses twenty-four to forty-eight laptops. Unfortunately these carts are often booked solid, in need of service, or lacking in technical support. About 10 percent of schools have loaner laptops that students may use for short periods of time (Wells and Lewis 2006), but these are most often located in media centers away from classrooms. As a result, the promise of integrated laptops and true mobile computing remains, even in 2008, unfulfilled at K–12 schools.

To address this shortcoming, a handful of states—Maine, Michigan, Pennsylvania, New Mexico, New Hampshire, and North Dakota—have provided their students with laptops in recent years. All 17,000 seventh graders in Maine, for example, were given new laptops at the beginning of 2003—an initiative that has now expanded to include state high schools. In a case study of a participating high school, teachers and students reported the laptop program had improved technology literacy among staff and students, increased access to educational resources, raised student motivation and interest in school, and fostered better interaction between teachers and students ("One-to-One Laptops" 2004). But recent economic conditions have led states to reconsider these promising programs. Our home state of Michigan, for instance, discontinued its planned laptop program in 2006 due to budget constraints.

Despite the relative scarcity of real mobile computing in K–12 schools today, we believe the day is coming—soon—when every student will have a laptop, purchased independently or provided by the state. Even as we write this book, laptops are becoming increasingly affordable. The Maine initiative, for example, supplied students with three-hundred-dollar laptops, and the Massachusetts Institute of Technology is partnering with Google and other corporations to develop a hundred-dollar laptop for the world's most impoverished countries.

Wireless Classrooms: Our Predictions

We anticipate that classrooms will be designed around the idea of mobile computing, like the EEL at Western Michigan University. With wireless connectivity, this laboratory has all of the power of a traditional computer lab but no stationary desktop computers and large monitors to look over or around. Desks in this classroom are not in fixed rows, there are no electrical wires or cables to trip over, and students can see and communicate with one another and the teacher just as they would in a regular classroom. Yet all of the power and possibility of the Internet is instantly accessible, and the classroom can change shape at a moment's notice to accommodate lectures, large-group discussion, small-group collaboration, and individual projects. The laptops may be closed or put away, and when they are the room looks and functions like any other classroom. This kind of flexible structure makes the classroom appealing to teachers regardless of how often they integrate the laptops into their teaching.

In this wireless classroom, all of the applications we have discussed in this book—text archives, threaded discussions, blogs, podcasts, feed readers, virtual worlds, class websites, and class blogs—become even more effective, especially when knowledgeable teachers weave these and other Web-based tools into student learning. When his students explore his online African literature syllabus, for example, Allen uses the wireless laptop classroom as a collaborative workshop space—splitting his students into small teams, with each group using a single laptop to explore and discuss sites with rich and challenging content. In this arrangement, Allen can review online resources with the data projector, and in the same way his students may also patch into the projector to show what they have been looking at. The whole-class can consider (with the teacher's help) how to understand, think critically about, and engage with online resources.

The workshoplike flexibility of the wireless classroom also allows students to learn at their own pace. In teaching website design, for instance, Allen has discovered that directing students through a step-by-step process is frustrating, inevitably leaving some students behind while slowing others down. So after the briefest of introductions, he moves away from whole-class instruction and turns the students loose to work on their own and in small groups. Tech-savvy students are free to move around the room to help others, but if all students are novices a tech expert (typically a student) may be invited to the class for a few meetings to help those who encounter problems. The laptops facilitate students working on their own project and getting help from their classmates at the same time. And since there are no fixed rows or tall machines to block the view, it is easy for Allen to see which students are on task and which students need help.

Teaching literature in this classroom, Allen's students can move smoothly between reading texts online, discussing them, and writing about them. Questions that come up during discussion can be googled by one or more students and, in seconds, additional information can be added to enrich the conversation. Since all of the laptops are connected wirelessly to the data projector, students can instantly share what they are reading or writing with the whole class. Students or the teacher can zoom in or out on the screen, point, comment, and interpret text and images, sound files, and video clips. Working in small groups, Allen's students explore ideas and write collaboratively, using wikispaces or Google Documents (a Web-based word-processing application), discussing the ideas and modifications as they simultaneously appear on each student's individual computer. Students work in rapid succession, discovering their thinking together, and developing skills in the classroom that they can continue to use when they collaborate from home or the library. The seamless integration of the Internet into teaching and learning in the English classroom becomes a model of the collaborative workplace.

A class blog is also readily integrated into a wireless laptop laboratory. Indeed, as the Web continues its movement toward 2.0 tools—online applications that let users create, share, and organize content like never before—the ideal classroom will allow our students to take advantage of these tools. And while Rob does not currently teach in such a classroom, he can envision how his blog would work there. Students might explore the course resources at Secondary Worlds individually or in small groups, for example, while being monitored for progress and understanding. They might watch the Google Reader screencast and then set up their own Google Reader accounts, with more advanced students assisting those who are struggling. Students could view video embedded in a class blog and write a responses on their own academic blogs, read posts on classmates' blogs and respond with comments, record and edit podcasts with two or three other classmates, write a collaborative interpretations of course texts, and much more.

We have concluded each chapter in this book with a small chart illustrating how the technology applications we have described may be used to meet the four goals of literature instruction that we described in our introduction. The chart we include as Figure 5–5 looks slightly different, simply because we

FIGURE 5–5 *Activities for the technology-enriched English classroom*

Use a class website or class blog to	Publish course syllabi and link to other syllabi of similar courses
	Link to text archives, databases, and other online resources
	Post course assignments and link to examples
	Link to threaded discussion forums
	Link to literary simulations within virtual realities
	Link to student book blogs or academic blogs
	Discuss current issues and articles related to English studies
	Highlight or publish exemplary student work
	Provide screencast tutorials
	Publish student podcasts
	Model effective technology integration in English language arts

believe that the two key applications we describe in this chapter—the classroom website and the classroom blog—encompass nearly all of the technologies discussed in this book. Our final chart, then, illustrates how we have used the class website and the class blog to integrate these applications, establishing our own Web presence in the technology-enriched English classroom.

We hope that our evocation of the wireless English classroom has not implied that laptops are necessary for you to establish a Web presence through a class website or a class blog. On the contrary, we know that the tools we have described in this book can work in classrooms with a single instructor station and data projector (see our suggestions at the end of this chapter for using class websites and class blogs with limited or no technology). But we also believe that wireless classrooms are just around the corner, and that many of us will find ourselves teaching in these environments within a few short years. One recent study of the nation's largest school districts, for example, found that 25 percent of the thousand respondents already had one-to-one laptop programs, and 50 percent of the respondents anticipated achieving one-to-one computing by 2011 (Hu 2007). Though skepticism has sometimes accompanied these programs—teachers and professors know that there is no such thing as quick fix and some hold that *laptops* has become just another educational buzzword—we hope that this book offers theoretically rich ways to use Web tools in your literature classroom, whether it is wireless or not. In all of your efforts to integrate Web technology—sometimes squeezing it into places where it had not been before—we encourage playing the believing game, which for us means hoping, even trusting, that the teachers like you will integrate technology into your classrooms in creative new ways that surpass our suggestions here.

Using Class Websites and Class Blogs with Limited or No Technology Resources

Class websites and class blogs can be effective platforms in rooms with limited technology. The great variety of resources we link to from our sites are still useful when displayed for the entire class on a data projector. In many situations, in fact, it is preferable to hold the attention of the entire class on a single site rather than letting students explore resources on their own.

- Teachers in one-computer classrooms can also require students to examine the class site or class blog from their home or from library or resource center computers, asking them to reply to a threaded discussion topic or post a blog entry as homework.

- If no technology resources are available at school or home, we still like the idea of teacher presence, even if this means approximating some of the effects of a class blog or site on a bulletin board. A teacher might post a paper profile of herself at the center of a bulletin board, and then surround the profile with information that is relevant to the class—previous student work, important articles, key terms or ideas, photographs of students or important images, and more. The main idea, we think, is to approximate the function and feel of a website or blog, drawing on the familiarity with these forms that most students already possess.

Web Resources Mentioned in Chapter 5

Allen Webb's Site (www.allenwebb.net) includes his African literature syllabus and other course materials described in this chapter.

Google Pages (www.pages.google.com) is a free online tool that makes it very easy to publish professional-looking webpages. Google supplies dozens of attractive templates and a very simple interface. Webpages are published at http://username.googlepages.com/home.

Google Reader (www.reader.google.com) is a free, Web-based RSS aggregator. Like all things Google, Google Reader has a clean design and is simple to use. Google Reader requires a Google account, which is also free. Google Reader is even more powerful when used in conjunction with Google News.

Literature Circles (www.literaturecircles.com) is a support resource for teachers using student-led book discussion groups in their classrooms. Sponsored by the Walloon Institute and Stenhouse Publishing, the site features book recommendations, classroom management strategies, and links to additional resources.

Secondary Worlds (www.secondaryworlds.com) is Robert Rozema's blog, which he uses as a teaching tool in his English education methods courses at Grand Valley State University.

Teaching English Through Technology (www.wmich.edu/teach english) was developed by the English education program at Western Michigan University in support of its Wireless English Education Laboratory. The site was designed to offer pre-service and in-service English teachers a range of strategies for technology integration.

Windows Media Encoder (www.microsoft.com/windows/windows media/forpros/encoder/default.mspx) is a free software application that allows you to capture movies of your computer screen. This tool is ideal for creating technology tutorial screencasts.

Wordpress is a free blogging application that may be installed on a school server (www.wordpress.org) or hosted by Wordpress (www.wordpress .com). Of the thousands of commercial blogging services, Wordpress is among the best, providing hundreds of professional themes, no advertisements, and many helpful features such as password protection and content syndication.

Conclusion

Becoming a Web Advocate:
Resistance, Rights, and Mentorship

Robert Rozema and Allen Webb

D eveloping Web tools and integrating them effectively into teaching is, like English teaching itself, a process of lifelong learning. We hope that *Literature and the Web* has inspired you to try new technologies in support of the teaching you already do. Beyond this most basic ambition, we also hope that you will become a Web advocate in your department, your school, your district, and beyond. For us, being Web advocates means knowing how to overcome the resistance that technology-based projects sometimes generate. Web advocacy also entails knowing your digital rights and responsibilities, as well as those of your students. And finally—and most importantly—being a Web advocate means mentoring those around you, assisting them in their efforts to integrate Web tools and resources into their English methods and curricula. We hope that this conclusion gives you practical ways of achieving these goals.

▓ Overcoming Resistance to Technology Integration

As enthusiastic as we are about the technology-enriched literature classroom, we know that many teachers encounter resistance when they attempt to integrate the tools, resources, and strategies we have discussed in this book. As we have worked to advocate Web technology at workshops and conferences throughout the country, we have heard too many stories from teachers who have been frustrated in their attempts to bring innovative Web applications into their classrooms. Teachers like Laura, who objected to her school's restrictive filtering software but did not know how to approach her principal. Teachers like Tom, whose hope to use student blogs was frustrated when a group of parents challenged his choice to "use dangerous sites like MySpace at school." And teachers like Jane, who wanted to try *Second Life* with her sophomores but was denied when her school's technology administrator realized the program required a reconfiguration of the network firewall. As these cases illustrate, resistance to Web technology may come from parents who fear for the safety of their children, from teaching colleagues who feel that technology threatens traditional education, from underinformed administrators who only know what they see in the news, or even from network administrators more concerned with security than student learning.

One strategy for dealing with resistance is simple: ask for help. Many English teachers lack training and expertise in technology, and so identifying supportive people—such as designated technology experts, colleagues, and even students—can be a great help developing new ideas and projects. If you are unable to find support in your building or district, remember that teachers who have undertaken technology experiments are often accessible via email and willing to mentor new adopters.

When dealing with administrators it is good to have information about the software and hardware requirements, the security risks posed to the school, and the logistics of implementing your project in your class. Technology mentors can help provide this information. It may also be convincing to colleagues, administrators, or parents to show that the particular approach or application has been used successfully in schools or universities elsewhere. Pointing to existing sites or displaying these examples can work to demonstrate the value of your project. And of course, we hope the examples and approaches described in this book become useful illustrations as you plan and implement your ideas.

If you still encounter resistance to a technology-based project, remember that technology is always changing, so something that seems implausible now may be feasible in a short time. Using new Web applications requires a willingness to experiment and the persistence to not give up after one try. Some applications that require expensive software and hardware today—such as *Second Life*—will likely become more accessible in the near future. If your grand idea proves to be unworkable, try something smaller. Instead of every student keeping an individual blog on the school server, you might publish a class blog on a commercial server where students could post their comments. Small-scale experiments can develop your own expertise and serve as examples to show to skeptics. Most technology administrators are more willing to let teachers use commercial or open-source Web applications such as Nicenet, Wordpress, Wikispaces, or Google Pages than to install similar applications on the school server.

Much of the resistance to Web-based projects results from misinformation generated by the media: the Web does receive a lot of positive press, but it is also frequently condemned as dangerous for students or inappropriate for school use. These negative portrayals can hurt our chances to integrate Web applications into our teaching. The scare over MySpace, for example, led to legislation that would ban social networking sites from public schools—taking many blogging services, instant messaging platforms, and other useful applications along with it. Some public schools have even hired detectives to warn their students of the risks of MySpace. The result is a constituency of scared parents, teachers, administrators, and even legislators who raise alarms and make snap decisions. To counter this effect, we recommend sharing technology success stories with parents, colleagues, and administrators; passing along articles that detail interesting technology-based projects; publishing student technology projects to the Web; and bringing in professional speakers who advocate meaningful technology use. Allen and I have discovered the effectiveness of the soft sell: we begin with the premise that technology reinforces what good teachers already practice—and avoid exaggerated claims that technology by itself radically reinvents teaching and learning.

We have also learned from our fellow teachers about the discussion over appropriate Web use and intellectual freedom. In 2006, at the NCTE national conference, we organized a session on "Civil Liberties and the New Technologies" that attracted many passionate teachers. Our experience led us to set forward basic principles that we believe English teachers should defend—rights and responsibilities that, while moderate, are nevertheless too frequently challenged.

Internet Rights and Responsibilities

The Web is an enormously powerful tool for learning and communication. As this book has illustrated, the possibilities for extending the curriculum, for developing student reading and writing, and for communicating and sharing ideas are extraordinary. How to teach students to use the Internet responsibly is a topic worthy of a book in its own right, and responsible use is obviously defined differently in the public schools (where the majority of students are minors) than in universities (where students are over eighteen and considered adults). Moreover the topic of teaching literature always generates concerns about appropriateness, teacher and student responsibility, and intellectual freedom. It is not surprising, then, that we find ourselves on the same ground—and sometimes the same thin ice—when we use the Web to enrich our teaching of literature.

Responding to legal mandates and common sense, schools and universities have created acceptable use policies governing access to online information. The great majority of schools use filtering software to control the sites that students visit, for instance—though such software frequently fails to distinguish between appropriate and inappropriate content. Concerns, sometimes based on media sensationalism, have also led legislatures and administrators to make decisions about access to the Internet. These decisions, we believe, should never be made at the cost of the following principles:

1. Teachers are in a better position to evaluate the appropriateness of Web resources and activities than administrators, legislatures, or others removed from the classroom. Respect for teacher decision making should be a starting point for technology integration in schools and universities.

2. Teaching with the Web means paying attention to what students are doing online. Long before computers existed, students passed notes to their friends, read comic books instead of their textbooks, or brought cheat sheets into examinations. Today students try to get away with updating their Facebooks during class, reading Web sites that are off topic, or text messaging answers to test questions. Teachers were responsible for appropriate classroom behavior before computers and they need to be responsible for appropriate classroom behavior after computers. This means giving clear directions and guidelines for activities, circulating and observing students, and turning computers off when they are not needed.

3. Becoming educated in the twenty-first century entails learning how to read and evaluate online information resources and learning how to write and communicate in digital genres. Denied the full range of reading and writing experiences offered by the Web, students are disadvantaged in the job market, which demands digital literacy from its workforce; muted in our democracy, whose public debate and political discourse have migrated to the Web; and excluded from the global community, which communicates and interconnects through digital networks.

4. Students have the right to read and evaluate information on the Web. The existence of pornography, hate, or misinformation on the Web should not

prevent students of all ages from benefiting from valuable and appropriate Internet sites, just as the existence of sexually explicit magazines should not exclude students from reading magazines. Moreover it is essential that young people learn to select the best resources that the Web makes available, developing the discernment necessary for their future reading lives. Since adult citizens in a democracy have a right to read materials, including websites, that may be politically or morally offensive to others, students in school need to be educated about how to think carefully and critically about their own beliefs and those of others as they are prepared to enter into society.

5. Students have the right to publish their writing to the Web and to communicate in digital media. Publishing and communicating online are powerful acts, and students must learn how to do so with due caution and common sense. Teachers must educate students about the risks of disclosing confidential information, the potential injuries in libeling others in public, and the rules and procedures of copyright. While course management systems such as Blackboard allow students to publish and communicate in a private online environment, lessons about these responsibilities—as well as lessons about audience, purpose, and voice—may be most persuasive in publicly accessible spaces.

There are many additional resources for teachers who wish to learn more about student rights and responsibilities in a digital age, and we have compiled a short list of these in the Web resources section of this chapter.

▓ Mentoring

Technology integration requires experimentation and practice. To gain expertise, teachers who are new to the Web should seek out supportive faculty members and technology specialists. We believe that you, as a reader of this book, are positioned to become a mentor of other teachers. After you have experimented with Web applications in your literature classroom and observed your students using new tools in imaginative ways, you may find yourself beginning conversations with your colleagues during lunch break or after school. Even in this informal way, you are becoming a mentor—shifting your role from seeking help to helping others.

Both of us can tell stories about finding the mentors we needed at specific times. When Allen designed his first webpages, a student was willing to come to his house, sit beside him for several hours, and show him the basic steps he needed to follow. When Rob was learning to use the MOO application, he met frequently online with an expert programmer who took the time to answer his questions about how to make the program work for his purposes. Both of us joined a special interest group of NCTE, the Assembly on Computers in English, where we would listen to classroom teachers—who seemed to us technology wizards—tell stories about their approaches and experiences.

While we began with experiments in our own classes, our fellow teachers were soon turning to us with questions and asking for our help. Shortly after Rob published his first class website in the late 1990s, for instance, he was recruited to lead a school workshop on the topic. Since then he has helped colleagues set up blogs, produce podcasts, record and edit video, create hypertext poems, and more. Allen has had similar successes in informal mentoring. We have both become known as technology experts in our respective departments, and this has become an enjoyable part of our teaching lives.

Mentoring students in Web technologies can also be incredibly rewarding. One of Rob's most fulfilling experiences as an English education professor came when two of his students presented at a regional conference. Rob had pushed his students to explore the academic possibilities of social networking sites, and two of his students rose to the challenge, developing MySpace profiles for literary characters from two novels—*Jake Reinvented* by Gordon Korman and *The Great Gatsby* by F. Scott Fitzgerald. In their presentation, David and Bethany showed how MySpace can help readers understand the complex social relationships between characters.

Beyond informal mentoring of colleagues and students, we also encourage you to take on more official roles in professional organizations. We moved from being active listeners in meetings of the Assembly on Computers in English to become workshop leaders ourselves. Rob became chair of the organization and orchestrates regular meetings in *Second Life*. Allen won significant grants involving preparing and organizing colleagues to use technology in their teaching. Both of us began presenting at conferences and in-service trainings. These opportunities allowed us to reach a broader audience of literature teachers and professors and to continue learning about emerging technologies.

We are excited about the new teaching journeys you are embarking on and we want to hear from you about your experiments and discoveries. We hope you will communicate with us—we're easy to find—and collaborate with us as you move from work in your own classroom to mentoring others. Bringing literature *and* the Web together creates new possibilities and new adventures. As Lewis in Shakespeare's *King John* says, "The day shall not be up so soon as I, to try the fair adventure of tomorrow."

Web Resources on Digital Rights and Responsibilities

American Civil Liberties Union (ACLU) (www.aclu.org) has resources for addressing Internet free speech; also see their information on privacy and technology (www.aclu.org/privacy).

American Library Association (www.ala.org) has a wealth of materials to support Internet access in libraries.

Computer Professionals for Social Responsibility (www.cpsr.org) is a global organization dedicated to responsible use of computer technology. It has helpful resources on privacy, civil liberties, open-source initiatives, and intellectual property.

Electronic Frontier Foundation (www.eff.org) is an organization that provides information about protecting freedom of speech on the Web. See especially their pages on student blogging (http://www.eff.org/bloggers/lg/faq-students.php) and on Internet filtering in schools (www.eff.org/Censorship/Censorware/net_block_report/).

NCTE Anti-Censorship Center (www.ncte.org/about/issues/censorship) has resources addressing traditional censorship, including nonprint materials and the Internet. Their statement "The Student's Right to Read" remains relevant in the digital age.

Northwest Educational Technology Consortium (www.netc.org/planning/planning/aup.php) offers guidelines for and examples of acceptable-use policies.

Virginia Department of Education (www.pen.k12.va.us/VDOE/Technology/AUP/home.shtml) has created a useful acceptable-use policy handbook.

Works Cited

"11 U.S. Soldiers Court-Martialed for Crimes in Iraq." 2006. *Al Jazeera Magazine* 19 Oct. www.aljazeera.com.

ACHEBE, CHINUA. 2000. *Things Fall Apart*. New York: Anchor Books.

ALEXIE, SHERMAN. 1997. "The Farm." *The Raven Chronicles*. www.ravenchronicles.org/ raven/rvback/issues/0397/Alexie.htm.

Alive in Baghdad: Video Blogging from the Middle East. 2007. Podcast. http://alivein baghdad.org.

ANDERSON, M. T. 2002. *Feed*. Cambridge: Candlewick Press.

APPLEBEE, ARTHUR N. 1993. *Literature in the Secondary School: Studies of Curriculum and Instruction in the United States*. NCTE Research Report, No. 25. Urbana, IL: National Council of Teachers of English.

AUDEN, W. H. 1968. *Secondary Worlds: Essays*. New York: Random House.

BARRON, JIM. 2007. Front Page Podcast. *The New York Times*. www.nytimes.com/ services/xml/rss/nyt/podcasts/frontpage.xml.

BLOOD, REBECCA. 2002. *The Weblog Handbook: Practical Advice on Creating and Maintaining Your Blog*. Cambridge: Perseus.

BORGES, JORGE LUIS. 1969. "The Library of Babel." In *Ficciones*. Ed. Anthony Kerrigan. Trans. Anthony Bonner. New York: Grove Press.

BORJA, RHEA R. 2005. "State Support Varies Widely." *Education Week* 24 (35): 18.

BOWEN, KEVIN. 2003. "Marc Laidlaw Interview." *Planet Half-Life* 8 Sept. http://planet halflife.gamespy.com/View.php?view=Interviews.Detail&id=10.

BRADSHAW, TOM. 2004. *Reading at Risk: A Survey of Literary Reading in America*. Washington, D.C.: National Endowment for the Arts.

BRANSHARES, ANNE. 2003. *The Sisterhood of the Traveling Pants*. New York: Delacorte.

BRONTE, CHARLOTTE. 2006. *Jane Eyre*. New York: Penguin Classics.

BUGEJA, MICHAEL J. 2007. "Distractions in the Wireless Classroom." *Chronicle of Higher Education.* 26 January. http://chronicle.com/jobs/news/2007/01/2007012601c/careers.html.

BUSH, VANNEVAR. 2006. "As We May Think: 1945." *The Atlantic Monthly* 298 (Sept.): 55–57.

CARD, ORSON SCOTT. 1992. *Ender's Game.* New York: Tor.

CAREY-WEBB, ALLEN. 2001. *Literature and Lives: A Response-Based, Cultural Studies Approach to Teaching English.* Urbana, IL: National Council of Teachers of English.

CARLSON, SCOTT. 2000. "Universities Find Wireless Systems Bring Them Convenience and Savings." *Chronicle of Higher Education* 11 Oct. http://chronicle.com/free/2000/10/2000101101t.htm.

CARVIN, ANDY. 2007. *Learning.now: At the Crossroads of Internet Culture and Education.* Public Broadcasting Service. Weblog. www.pbs.org/teachers /learning.now.

CHBOSKY, STEPHEN. 1999. *The Perks of Being a Wallflower.* New York: Pocket Books.

CONRAD, JOSEPH. 1990. *Heart of Darkness.* New York: Dover Thrift.

CORMIER, ROBERT. 1986. *The Chocolate War.* New York: Laurel-Leaf Books.

"Court Martial in Iraq Rape Case." 2006. *BBC News* 19 October. http://news.bbc.co.uk/2/hi/americas/6064444.stm.

DANIELS, HARVEY. 2002. *Literature Circles: Voice and Choice in Book Clubs and Reading Groups.* 2nd ed. Portland, ME: Stenhouse.

DEAN, ZOEY. 2003. *The A-List.* New York: Little Brown and Company.

DEFOE, DANIEL. 2005. *Moll Flanders.* New York: Signet Classics.

DIEM, ROBERT. 2007. *The Daily Idiom.* Podcast. www.learnoutloud.com.

ECKERT, LISA SCHADE. 2006. *How Does It Mean? Engaging Reluctant Readers Through Literary Theory.* Portsmouth, NH: Heinemann.

Educational Podcasting Network. 2007. http://epnweb.org.

FIZTGERALD, F. SCOTT. 2004. *The Great Gatsby.* New York: Scribner.

"Four U.S. Soldiers Charged with Rape and Murder." 2006. *CNN* 18 Oct. www.cnn.com/2006/LAW/10/18/soldiers.court/index.html.

FOX, ERIN. 2005. "Tracking U.S. Trends." *Education Week* 24 (35): 40.

FULTON, KATHLEEN, and ROBERT SIBLEY. 2003. "Barriers to Digital Equity." In *Toward Digital Equity: Bridging the Divide in Education.* Ed. Solomon, Gwen, et al. Boston: Allyn and Bacon.

GIBSON, WILLIAM. 1984. *Neuromancer.* New York: Ace Science Fiction.

GOLDING, WILLIAM. 1997. *Lord of the Flies.* New York: Riverhead Books.

GREG. 2003. "Prediction Watch: The Prescience of Orson Scott Card." Weblog. *Begging to Differ.* 15 July. www.beggingtodiffer.com.

GROSSMAN, LEV. 2005. "Larger Than Life: Novelist of the Screen." *Time* 165 (21): 57.

———. 2006. "Person of the Year: You." *Time* 168 (26): 38.

Grunwald Associates. 2003. *Connected to the Future: A Report on Children's Internet Use from the Corporation for Public Broadcasting, 2002.* www.cpb.org/stations/reports/connected.

HARDING, JAMES. 2006. "Google Does Book Reading a Huge Favor." *New York Times* 31 August. http://business.timesonline.co.uk/tol/business/columnists/article623550 .ece.

HICKS, TROY. 2007. *Digital Writing, Digital Teaching*. Weblog. www.hickstro.org.

HU, WINNIE. 2007. "Seeing No Progress, Some Schools Drop Laptops." *New York Times* 4 May. www.nytimes.com/2007/05/04/education/04laptop.html.

HUXLEY, ALDOUS. 1998. *Brave New World*. New York: Harper Perennial.

ISBEN, HENRIK. 1965. *A Doll's House*. New York: Penguin Classics.

KAJDER, SARA, et al. 2004. "A Space for 'Writing Without Writing': Blogs in the Language Arts Classroom." *Learning and Leading with Technology* 31 (6): 32.

KORMAN, GORDON. 2003. *Jake Reinvented*. New York: Hyperion.

LEE, HARPER. 1988. *To Kill a Mockingbird*. New York: Harper Collins.

LENHART, AMANDA, MARY MADDEN, and PAUL HITLIN. 2005. *Teens and Technology: Youth Are Leading the Transition to a Fully Wired and Mobile Nation*. Pew Internet and American Life Project. 27 July. www.pewInternet.org/pdfs/PIP_Teens_Tech_ July2005 Web.pdf.

MARRIOTT, MICHEL. 2006. "Blacks Turn to Internet Highway, and Digital Divide Starts to Close." *New York Times* 31 March. www.nytimes.com/2006/03/31/us/ 31divide.html.

McGANN, JEROME. 2004. *Radiant Textuality: Literature After the World Wide Web*. New York: Palgrave Macmillan.

MILTON, JOHN. 1971. *Paradise Lost*. Ed. Alastair Fowler. Harlow: Longman.

MOMADAY, N. SCOTT. 1976. *The Way to Rainy Mountain*. Albuquerque: University of New Mexico Press.

MOURSUND, DAVID, and TALBOT BIELEFELDT. 1999. *Will New Teachers Be Prepared to Teach in a Digital Age? A National Survey on Information Technology in Teacher Education*. International Society for Technology in Education and Milken Family Foundation.

MURRAY, JANET H. 1998. *Hamlet on the Holodeck: The Future of Narrative in Cyberspace*. Cambridge: MIT Press.

MYERS, WALTER DEAN. 2001. *Monster*. New York: Amistad Press.

OGLES, JACOB. 2005. "Keyboard Is Mightier than Sword." *Wired Magazine News* 31 March. www.wired.com/news/culture/games/0,67008-0.html.

"One-to-One Laptops in a High School Environment: Piscataquis Community High School Study Final Report." 2004. Mitchell Institute and Bill and Melinda Gates Foundation.

OPPENHEIMER, TODD. 2003. *The Flickering Mind: The False Promise of Technology in the Classroom, and How Learning Can Be Saved*. New York: Random House.

ORTIZ, JUDITH. 1996. *An Island Like You*. New York: Puffin.

ORWELL, GEORGE. 1950. *1984*. New York: Signet.

OWENSON, MORGAN SYDNEY. 1986. *The Wild Irish Girl: A National Tale*. New York: Pandora.

PARRY, DAVID. 2006. "The Technology of Reading and Writing in the Digital Space: Why RSS Is Crucial for a Blogging Classroom." *Blogs for Learning*. Weblog. Michigan State University. http://blogsforlearning.msu.edu/articles/view. php?id=6.

PARSAD, BASMAT, et al. 2005. *Internet Access in U.S. Public Schools and Classrooms: 1994–2003*. Washington, D.C.: National Center for Education Statistics.

Perseus Development Corporation. 2005. "The Blogging Geyser: Blogs Blast from 31.6 Million Today to Reach 53.4 Million by Year End." http://perseus.com/survey/news/releases/release_blogginggeyser.html.

Podcast Bangladesh. 2007. Podcast. http://feeds.feedburner.com/PodcastBangladesh.

POPE, ROB. 2006. *Textual Intervention: Critical and Creative Strategies for Literary Studies*. New York: Routledge.

PURVES, ALAN C., et al. 1995. *How Porcupines Make Love: Readers, Texts, Cultures in the Response-Based Literature Classroom*. White Plains: Longman Publishers.

RICHARDSON, WILL. 2003. "Weblogs in the English Classroom: More Than Just Chat." *English Journal* 93 (1): 39.

———. 2006. *Blogs, Wikis, and Podcasts and Other Powerful Web Tools for the Classroom*. Thousand Oaks: Corwin Press.

———. 2007. *Weblogg-ed: The Read/Write Web in the Classroom*. Weblog. www. Weblogg-ed.com.

ROSENBLATT, LOUISE M. 1978. *The Reader, the Text, the Poem: The Transactional Theory of the Literary Work*. Carbondale, IL: Southern Illinois UP.

———. 1995. *Literature as Exploration*. 5th ed. New York: Modern Language Association of America.

ROZEMA, ROBERT. 2007. *Secondary Worlds*. Weblog. http://secondaryworlds.com.

ROZEMA, ROBERT, et al. 2007. *YA! Cast*. Podcast. 8 March 2007. http://phobos.apple.com/WebObjects/MZStore.woa/wa/viewPodcast?id=207669929.

SELINGO, JEFFREY. 2004. "In the Classroom, Web Logs Are the New Bulletin Boards." *The New York Times* 19 August.

SEWARD, SAMUEL SWAYZE. 1909. Ed. *Narrative and Lyric Poems for Students*. New York: Holt.

SHAKESPEARE, WILLIAM. 1998. *A Midsummer Night's Dream*. New York: Signet Classics.

———. 1998. *Macbeth*. New York: Signet Classics.

———. 1998. *Much Ado About Nothing*. New York: Signet Classics.

———. 1998. *The Tempest*. New York: Signet Classics.

———. 2004. *King John*. New York: Signet Classics.

Shakespeare by Another Name. 2007. Podcast. http://shakespearebyanothername.com/feed.xml.

STEINBECK, JOHN. 1993. *Of Mice and Men*. New York: Penguin Books.

———. 2006. *The Grapes of Wrath*. New York: Penguin Classics.

STEPHENSON, NEAL. 1992. *Snow Crash*. New York: Bantam Books.

STOLL, CLIFFORD. 1995. *Silicon Snake Oil: Second Thoughts on the Information Highway*. New York: Doubleday.

SWANSON, CHRISTOPHER B. 2006. "Tracking U.S. Trends." *Education Week* 25 (35): 50.

TAPSCOTT, DONALD. 1998. *Growing Up Digital: The Rise of the Net Generation*. New York: McGraw-Hill.

This I Believe Podcast. 2007. Podcast. National Public Radio. http://thisibelieve.org.

TOLKIEN, J. R. R. 1966. *The Tolkien Reader*. New York: Ballantine Books.

TYSON, LOIS. 2001. *Learning for a Diverse World: Using Critical Theory to Read and Write About Literature*. New York: Routledge.

WEILER, GREG. 2003. "Using Weblogs in the Classroom." *English Journal* 92 (5): 73.

WELLS, JOHN, and LAURIE LEWIS. 2006. *Internet Access in U.S. Public Schools and Classrooms: 1994–2005*. Washington, D.C.: National Center for Education Statistics.

WILDE, OSCAR. 1998. *The Importance of Being Earnest*. New York: Oxford.

WILHELM, JEFFREY D. 1997. *You Gotta BE the Book: Teaching Engaged and Reflective Reading with Adolescents*. New York: Teachers College Press.

WRIGHT, RICHARD. 1998. *Native Son*. New York: HarperCollins.

Index

Brashares, Ann, 65
Brave New World (Huxley), 64, 87–94, 103
Brecht, Bertold, 13
British and Irish Poetry, 3, 24
Bronte, Charlotte, 39–41
Bush, Vannevar, 21
Butcher, Samuel, 8
Butler, Samuel, 8

Carey-Webb, Allen, xvii
Card, Orson Scott, 51–52
Carvin, Andy, 117
Chbosky, Steven, 57–60, 72
Chekhov, Anton, 12
Chapman, John, 7–8
Chaucer, Geoffrey, xvi
The Chocolate War (Cormier), 67, 120
Clark, Gillian, 3
Class web site
    as syllabus, 107–113
    for class activities, 110–112
    for class content, 107–110
    creating and publishing, 112–113
    in the technology-enriched English class-
        room, 125
    listing other syllabi on, 111–112
    with limited or no technology resources,
        126–127
CNN, 13–14
Close reading, xv–xvi, 5, 7 , 14, 20, 23, 47,
    73, 96, 97
Cofer, Judith Ortiz, 103
CoLearn, 46
Collins, Billy, 3, 61
Comicvine, 74, 78
Computer Professionals for Social Responsi-
    bility, 135
Conrad, Joseph, xvi
Contexts, social, historical, and cultural,
    xii–xiii, xvi–xviii, 7, 20, 38, 44–45,
    47–48, 60–61, 73, 95–97, 102, 109
Cormier, Robert, 67, 120
Cowper, William, 3
Creative Commons, 63, 77

Daily Idiom Podcast, 63
Daniels, Harvey, 43, 55, 110–111
Dante, 19
Dean, Zoey, 65

Defoe, Daniel, 86, 103
del.icio.us, 74, 79
Desire2Learn, 33, 50
Devil on the Cross (Thiong'o), 44
Dick, Linda, 96
Dickens, Charles, 103
Dickinson, Emily, 3, 19
Digital Writing, Digital Teaching, 54, 114
Divine Comedy (Dante), 19
Donne, John, xv
DOPA, 53
"Dulce et Decorum Est" (Owen), 13
Dykema, Meghan, 103

Early English Books Online, 2
Eckert, Lisa Schade, xvii
Ed Blogger Praxis, 54, 76
Edublogs, 54, 76, 116
Educational Bloggers' Network, 54, 76
Educational Podcasting Network, 62, 77
Electronic discussions
    as tool for teacher reflection, 47
    class activities with, 34–36
    definition of, 32
    in the literature classroom, 47
    selecting, 32–33
    strategies for leading, 37–38
    teaching literature with, 39–43
    with limited or no technology resources,
        49
    with participants beyond the classroom,
        43–46
Electronic Frontier Foundation, 135
Elliot, T. S., xvi
enCore environment
    definition of, 81
    and *1984*, 81–85
    and *Brave New World*, 87–94
    and Literary Worlds, 86–87, 95–97
    discussing literature in, 91–95
    in higher education, 86
    in the literature classroom, 97
    introducing setting in, 83, 90–91
    role-playing as characters in, 84–85, 87–89
Ender's Game (Card), 51–52
English Education Laboratory, 121, 123
Epals, 45, 50
Essay mills. *See* Plagiarism.
EverQuest, 81, 86